THE WEAVER'S CRAFT

THE
WEAVER'S CRAFT

L. E. Simpson

B.A., F.Coll.H., Higher Froebel Certificate
Formerly Lecturer in Crafts at the University of Birmingham

M. Weir

Higher Froebel Certificate

THE DRYAD PRESS

Thirteenth Edition, 1978
85219 130 8

Published by The Dryad Press, Northgates, Leicester and printed in England
by Hemmings & Capey (Leicester) Ltd.

Foreword

AMONG the great crowds at a famous one-day Show a man stood watching as a spinner worked at her wheel and I wove on my handloom, outside the tent where the Buckinghamshire Guild of Weavers, Spinners and Dyers were showing. Many bystanders had shown interest, some crass ignorance, a few some background knowledge, but this man showed such familiarity with the craft and such intimate understanding of a loom that I downed tools and asked him about his experience as a weaver. His explanation was simple. 'I saw a handloom being worked at an Exhibition and it caught me. I bought a book, followed its instructions and built my own loom, and I have woven in my spare time ever since. It is a good book'. 'And what was the book?' I asked. '*The Weaver's Craft*, by Simpson & Weir', said he.

What a tribute to a book designed to teach the art and practice of weaving! But his is by no means the only case of the kind that has come to my notice during many long years of weaving, teaching and inspecting schools. Over and over again since this book came out in its first edition over thirty years ago, I have been told of its value by people far from skilled advice or unable to attend classes of instruction. They have been enabled at least to start on the long road that is the weaver's path to success, or to delve in the book for some piece of technical knowledge or the solution of an unexpected problem. Many teachers and their pupils owe a debt to the authors of this book, and in many cases the notable additions and improvements in this ninth edition are the outcome of the friendly advice, criticism and questions of just such readers.

I use *The Weaver's Craft* frequently myself, both in my own weaving and in work with pupils, and am certain of its worth. There are many books on weaving and the allied processes which specialise in one direction or another. What is it that has given this particular book its enduring and valuable qualities? It is a very honest, and in my opinion, a very successful effort to put down in print the essential processes of this lovely craft, to analyse its stages and to work out possible courses of development to fit the needs of young and old, beginners and practised hands. With the dignity and worth of the craft always in mind, these teacher-authors continually relate its processes to their place in education.

I cannot speak of Mrs. Simpson and her work except by hearsay. I only met her briefly once or twice but I know from others how great has been the loss caused by her early death and how fine the courage that has enabled her sister, Mrs. Weir, to go on with the work alone.

I have known Mrs. Weir for many years, both personally and as a skilled teacher and practical weaver—a staunch friend and colleague, generous in the help she is always ready to give others from her store of experience. Her qualities are reflected in this book. Differences of opinion over matters of colour, taste, design we might have, but never over the fundamental value of the craft nor over the teaching of children and the developing place weaving, spinning and dyeing should have in education.

These qualities are among those which have enabled her to see this work through, and I wish the book well-earned success. There is value in it for all weavers and all teachers of the weaver's craft.

J. MACK, O.B.E.,
H.M. Inspector of Schools (retired)
President, Buckinghamshire Guild of
Weavers, Spinners and Dyers.

Author's Foreword

IT IS MOST gratifying to the author that this book has stood the test of time and is still in demand not only in this country but in many parts of the world.

When originally written in 1932 there were on the market few English books dealing with the craft of weaving. Since then innumerable books, as indicated in the Bibliography, have been produced for the more advanced weaver.

The Weaver's Craft was never intended to be a mere text book of instructions but rather to outline the history of the craft from its earliest stages on primitive looms to the present form on the modern Table and Foot looms—of which there are a great many varieties on the market today. Pattern drafts were given merely as suggestions in the hope that weavers would adapt, improve and originate their own drafts and so make themselves familiar with the working of their looms.

In addition, the author hoped that users of the book would experiment with the numerous varieties of natural and synthetic materials now available, which offer unlimited scope to the more ambitious and venturesome weaver.

The author hopes that the new eleventh edition will continue to give help and encouragement to all who are anxious for the preservation and development of this ancient and beautiful craft.

M.W.

Acknowledgments

THE authors wish to express their gratitude to the following:

Messrs. Ernest Benn Ltd., for permission to reproduce a drawing from *Greek Vase Paintings*; G. R. Carline, Esq., of the Bankfield Museum, Halifax, and to the Royal Anthropological Institute for permission to reproduce drawings from *Primitive Looms*, G. Ling Roth.

Miss J. Mack, O.B.E., for kindly writing the Foreword.

Mrs. Mary Meigs Atwater for permission to use in this book Drafts Nos. 9, 14, 15, 18, 19, 21, 24, 25, 28, 35, 36, 39, 40–43, from her book, *The Shuttlecraft Book of American Hand-Weaving*, published by the Macmillan Company, of New York.

Miss Robinson, M.A., Head Mistress of Howell's School, Denbigh, for permission to use Figs. 21 and 22 from the School Magazine and for the loan of children's work illustrated in Fig. 24.

Miss McLeod, of the same school, for her help and co-operation.

The publishers of *Athene* for the loan of blocks, Figs. 21 and 22.

Eileen Van Tromp, of West Chiltington, for loan of samples Fig. 138 (circular bag) and Fig. 137 (raffia mat on cotton warp).

Mrs. K. Walker, of Bedford, for loan of samples of spaced warps, Figs. 136*a*, *b* and *c*.

Mr. A. Mann, of Chichester, for producing many of the photographs and for the samples of tweeds.

Students, teachers and other friends who have kindly lent samples.

Contents

CONTENTS

Illustrations

CHAPTER I
Introductory

RECENT years have witnessed a great revival of interest in the early crafts. Inspired, perhaps, in the first instance, by Ruskin and Morris, artists have lamented the mechanical perfection and the tendency to over-elaborate decoration of the machine-made product, and have endeavoured to open our eyes to the beauty of early craftsmanship—a beauty due to character and individuality in the finished article only possible when it has been conceived and executed throughout by the same person. Such work is simple and direct in execution, and its decoration is restrained through the limitations of the tools, whereas the complexity of modern machines makes over-elaborate and unsuitable decoration only too easy.

This interest, in the craft of weaving in particular, has proved to be by no means fleeting or confined to the few. Hand-loom weaving has been practised as a hobby, and as a means of livelihood, by an increasing number of people, and the public have shown a keen interest in their work and appreciation of the beauty of texture and colour in the fabrics produced. This change in public taste is, perhaps, even now reacting on the manufacturers, for many of the newer fabrics offered for sale in the shops seem to be more tasteful, and to reflect the influence of the hand-loom weaver in their textures and patterns.

The increasing realisation in the schools of the value of handicrafts in education, and by such organisations as the Women's Institutes of the value of hobbies and of creative activity for women, have all helped to increase the popularity of the weaving craft. Human nature has an inborn desire to create —a desire which has unfortunately during the past century of factory production and division of labour been unsatisfied for many, and allowed to lie dormant—but which, when permitted to work itself out, helps forward the development of the individual, and results in the most intense feeling of satisfaction. No form of creative activity produces this satisfaction to a more intense degree than the weaving process, because here most beautiful results can be produced from the crudest materials and the simplest of tools, merely by thoughtful work, taste, and patience, on the part of the weaver. Not every weaver, it is true, will begin with the rough fleece, though all should have some acquaintance with the spinning and dyeing processes; but the change from this simple fleece to the finished fabric, with its beauty of texture, and charm of colour and pattern, is as satisfying to the producer as it is astonishing to the onlooker.

In the age of the home crafts everyone was familiar with the methods by which the necessities of life were produced, but in these days the purchaser knows and cares little about the way in which things he buys have been made available for his use. Yet, when once attention has been attracted, everyone is interested in the way in which things are made. Farmers of the writers' acquaintance were astonished to find that such things as hand looms and spinning wheels still existed, and showed a genuine interest and pride in seeing fleece from their own farms converted into cloth ! This awakening of interest in the making of things leads to a sympathetic attitude towards work and workers, and an increased appreciation of the past work of man. The use of a simple loom enables the weaver to feel astonishment at the complications of the factory machine and an amazed admiration for the minds of men who evolved it. A weaver who has been taught how to make and put on a long warp of many threads cannot fail to wonder who first discovered the method which eliminates all possibility of tangles, and to marvel at the ingenuity of the human mind. This historical interest is ever present. The beginner working with coarse fibres on a simple frame loom reproduces the activity of the earliest weavers. Stage by stage comes the desire for variety in colour and pattern and the evolution of labour-saving devices. A course of weaving, worked out historically from the earliest and simplest to the later and more complex methods, gives a real understanding of the loom and its uses. It is also of interest to realise that primitive people of today use methods and appliances for weaving such as were used by early weavers many centuries ago.[1]

A worker on a hand loom must have an added sympathy with the weavers of times prior to the Industrial Revolution and a greater possibility of admiring the complexity of, if not *quite* understanding, the modern Jacquard loom. From the standpoint of education, weaving becomes a most valuable craft if treated in the way indicated above. There is a constant appeal to the intelligence of the pupil in the development of the craft from its simplest forms—in the making of looms, the invention of labour-saving devices, in the invention of patterns, and finally, in the understanding of methods and appliances already invented by others. In addition, the craft should do much to improve the standard of taste by giving experience in the arrangement of colours and patterns, appreciation of the simple beauty of hand-woven textures, and of the individuality of the hand-made fabric.

Weaving is a craft which can be practised by people of all ages. The six-year-old will enjoy weaving with strips of coloured paper, felt, raffia, or dyed tape. At different stages during school life various aspects of the craft will be of interest, and, for the adult worker, weaving on the traditional type of hand loom or on one of the many modern forms of table loom will prove a fascinating

---

[1] *Primitive Looms*, Ling Roth, and the collection of looms at the Bankfield Museum, Halifax.

a

b

c

FIG. 1.—THREE RAFFIA BAGS SHOWING SOUND CONSTRUCTION, GOOD HANDLES AND FASTENINGS.

a. Beach bag woven in red, black and natural raffia.

b. Handbag woven in beige, brown and natural raffia.

c. Shopping bag made from plaited raffia in natural colour.

and profitable hobby. The craft is an inexpensive one. Raw materials are not costly; there need be little, if any, waste; much can be accomplished with very simple equipment, and the finished articles are useful and saleable.

It is the aim of this book to give help to the weaver in no matter what branch of the work she may be interested. It should not be beneath the dignity of the most grown-up, however, to begin with simple things, for only in this way can a thorough understanding of the craft be developed. Children's work will not show the same mastery of technique and finish, but the simplest weaving with raffia on cardboard is capable of producing articles of beauty and charm worthy of the most skilful worker. Samples of more advanced work are shown in Fig. 1.

A wide experience in the teaching of crafts prompts the writers to intersperse the text with practical hints in the hope of helping teachers with some of the difficulties which may be encountered in teaching the craft to children. The book is not intended only for teachers, however, but for all who are interested in the pursuit of the craft, and the private weaver will doubtless condone and pass lightly over such parts as are not of immediate interest.

CHAPTER II

The Beginnings

"You can concentrate the history of mankind into the evolution of flax, cotton, and wool fibre into clothing."—DEWEY.

MENTION of the earliest weavers has been made in the previous chapter, and it is interesting and valuable for anyone taking up this craft to think a little about the beginnings of weaving.

It is easy to imagine our primitive ancestors endeavouring to make use of natural fibres such as rushes, grasses, and the long narrow leaves of palm-like plants by threading them in and out to form a fabric which might serve for mats and coverings. This very flexible material would be much more difficult to control than such things as twigs and branches, which had already been interlaced to make shields for the mouth of the cave and for other purposes. The worker would soon experience the need for some means of stretching one set of strands (the warp) while the others (the weft) were woven under and over.[1] One of the earliest methods adopted was to tie the warp strands to a low-hanging branch of a tree and to weight each strand by tying a stone on to the other end. This method of weighting the strands is seen in pictures of Greek looms (see above reproduction of Penelope's loom from a Greek vase painting), and these 'loom weights' (pear-shaped pieces of clay or lead) have

[1]It may be interesting in this connection to quote an experience with a class of seven-year-old children in a council school. They had had a series of lessons on Primitive Man, and were trying experiments in reproducing his activities in the direction of pottery making, sewing, 'bead threading', weaving, etc. In the effort to weave from green rushes mats for the cave they had made, the children themselves suggested working in pairs, A stretching out one set of rushes while B threaded the others in and out. These children rediscovered for themselves the need for some sort of 'loom', and were well on the way to inventing one for themselves.

4

been amongst the relics found during excavations in Greece, and are attributed to the fifth century B.C. Another method which would soon evolve would be to tie the lower ends to a broken-off branch resting on the ground, and from this would develop the plan of a separate frame made from four branches fastened into a rectangle, and used either vertically propped up against some support, or horizontally, the weaver sitting on the ground with the loom placed over his legs.

Beginners may experiment with such a frame made from four pieces of wood nailed together at the corners, or may find ready-made equipment such as old picture frames. The strands of raffia, rush, or other available material, may be tied separately to the upper and lower beams, and at a later stage, if the threads are long enough for continuous warping, they may be wound round nails placed at regular intervals along these beams (Fig. 2).

For the younger children, however, it may be well to use more sophisticated and more manageable material such as stiff paper, or strips of stout cloth or

FIG. 2.—Simple wooden frame with warp.

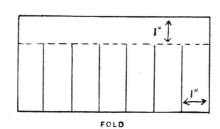

FOLD

FIG. 3a.—Cutting paper for mat.

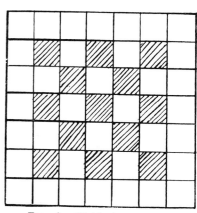

FIG. 3b.—Finished paper mat.

felt, or dyed tape, for their earliest efforts. The majority of six-year-old children quickly learn to thread 'under one and over one' and to reverse the process in alternate rows, but in some cases the task has presented enormous difficulty. The teacher should demonstrate clearly on a large scale with brightly coloured stiff paper, the children telling at each step what is to be done. A convenient form for these first attempts by young children is provided by a 7-inch square of stiff paper, together with five strips, each 6½ inches by 1 inch, of paper in contrasting colour. These materials may well be prepared by older children requiring practice in measurement. The square is folded into two, a line is drawn along the folded paper 1 inch from the two cut edges, and cuts are made at a distance of 1 inch apart from the fold to this line (Fig. 3a). The 1-inch

5

strips are then woven into this and the ends fastened underneath with a touch of paste (Fig. 3b). The tablecloth and mats illustrated in Fig. 8 can easily be made by children in the Infants' School and form excellent covers for their tables at lunch-time. For the cloths the 1-inch wide paper strips may be pinned on to a blackboard, wall or low table. When the weaving is finished the article is bordered on both sides by pasting a 2-inch strip cut from stiff paper.

An alternative method is to paste together the 2-inch wide strips to form three sides of a rectangle. Having placed this paper frame with the open side at the base, the 1-inch warp strips are then pasted to the inner edge of the top wide strip, and the weaving is started. As each row of weft is inserted it is pasted down to each of the side strips and so kept in place. When the weaving is complete the rectangle is finished by pasting on the remaining 2-inch border strip and then the whole of the border is lined.

The warp strands of stiff paper should always be placed very close together since the interlacing weft strands do not take up as much space as do those of other materials. Subsequent work may be done on a finer scale.

These early efforts should always have, for the young child, some purpose other than mere practice: the teacher may wish merely to teach a process, but the children are working mats for the doll's house, table mats for the lunch period, or for mother's use at home and such like. It is a good plan at this stage, for the sake of the children who find difficulty in learning the process, for the teacher to set up a co-operative piece of weaving in strips of coloured felt. A floor mat can be made on which children may sit during story telling or other periods. An old picture frame may be used, or the strips may be fastened with drawing-pins on to a board. These strips should be 1 inch wide, and a contrasting colour should be used for the weft. The teacher will demonstrate the weaving in of the first strips of weft, and then call on individual children to add a strip. The work can then be left for the children to continue at will in odd moments, but the teacher will make a point of spending a few minutes daily in helping such individuals as find it difficult.

After this introductory work, weaving with raffia, coarse cotton yarn—candlewick, or coarse wool may be attempted. The wooden frames already mentioned may be used, or the simple board loom (Fig. 4) which is mentioned again later in Chapter VI. A spacing gauge of wood or cardboard is used. At this stage the end of the warp may be attached by a nail or drawing-pin, or tied round the projecting edge of the board. The warp is then carried round and round the board, each strand lying in the notch of the spacer, and the end being secured in the same way as the beginning. A simpler and cheaper method is to use pieces of cardboard. These may be cut into a series of points at the upper and lower edges (Fig. 5). The warp is tied round the first point (A) at the top right-hand corner, carried down and round point B at lower right-hand

6

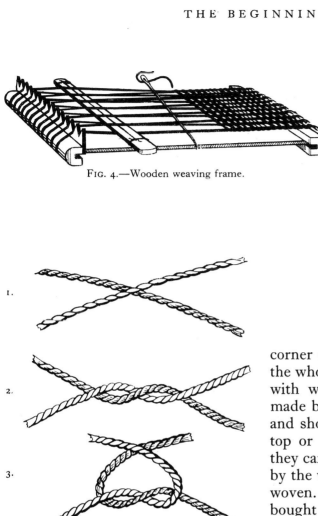

FIG. 4.—Wooden weaving frame.

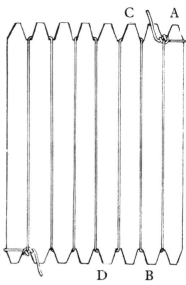

FIG. 5.—Cardboard frame for simple weaving.

1.

2.

3.

4.

5.

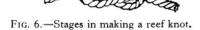

FIG. 6.—Stages in making a reef knot.

corner up to point C, and so on until the whole area to be woven is covered with warp strands. Joins should be made by means of *reef knots* (Fig. 6), and should preferably be kept at the top or bottom of the frame, though they can be fairly successfully covered by the weft if left in the portion to be woven. Such 'weaving frames' can be bought ready prepared from most educational supply firms, but it is better if the pupils make them for themselves. Unfortunately, this is rather a difficult task for children who would be quite capable of doing the weaving. It might well be done by older children in the same school, and would provide a useful exercise in measurement and the cutting of cardboard. Instead of making such looms, a simpler method may be adopted— the warp being threaded through holes pierced in the cardboard at a

7

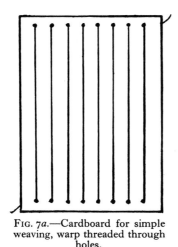

FIG. 7*a*.—Cardboard for simple weaving, warp threaded through holes.

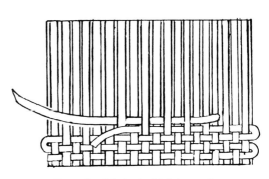

FIG. 7*b*.—Method of joining weft.

short distance from upper and lower edges (Fig. 7*a*). This enables the warp threads to be placed more closely together.

The Weaving.—This should be done with material of a different colour. The actual process has already been learned. It may be done with the fingers, or with the aid of a coarse blunt needle. A new difficulty now occurs in the control of the *tension* of the weft threads. Beginners invariably tend to pull these too tightly and so produce a 'waist' (Fig. 7*d*). Some people avoid this by placing a knitting needle or similar piece of thin metal or wood down each side of the work, round which the strand is taken at every 'return'. This is an undesirable 'prop', and the pupil should learn to control the tension without such mechanical aids. The strand should be bent sharply over at the extreme width of the warp before a return is made, and then must not be tightly pulled (Fig. 7*c*). It is easy to realise that in going under and over a number of warp strands

FIG. 7*c*.—Good weaving.

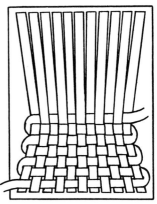

FIG. 7*d*.—Bad weaving, showing 'waist'.

FIG. 8.—TABLECLOTH AND MATS WOVEN IN STIFF PAPER.

some of the length of the weft is taken up, and allowance must be made for this.

Each strand should be pushed up and made level before the next is inserted. Raffia, nicely woven, produces a delightful texture unequalled by any other material, but in the early stages it is difficult for young children to acquire a technique which does not produce depressing results.

As the raffia strands are not long, joins will be necessary. To start a new strand, weave the old one as far as it will go, leaving its end at any point except the edges of the piece of work. Then, with the new strand, go back the width of five or six warp strands, and weave under and over the same strands as before (Fig. 7b). The two ends are left. The pressing up of subsequent rows makes them secure, and any projecting ends are snipped off afterwards.

It may be well to note that two different kinds of texture may result from the first attempts at weaving of this kind. If the warp is not too far apart (not less than 6 strands to the inch) and the weft not too closely pressed together, then an equal amount of warp and weft will show in the finished fabric, and as different colours have been used the result will be an even check. If, on the other hand, the warp threads are farther apart, and the weft very tightly packed, then the warp will not be seen in the finished fabric, which will be thick, and will show only the weft colour. This is not a desirable texture at this

FIG. 9.—AN OUTDOOR WEAVING CLASS.

stage, but will be useful and even necessary later, so no harm will be done if the pupils discover the possibility at this stage.

These plain pieces of weaving should never be regarded as mere practice. They may be used as floor mats for the doll's house or table mats, or may be sewn up to make tiny lunch bags, purses, needle cases, book covers, etc.

CHAPTER III

The Weaver as Artist

I. PATTERN

I T is not easy to decide whether the earliest decoration resulted from an innate sense of beauty, or whether it just happened through a desire for variety and an attempt to relieve the monotony of always doing the same thing. Anyone who has done a big piece of work, such as needlework or knitting, will remember the relief with which a new stage in the process, or the opportunity to use a different colour, was welcomed, and it is easy to believe that the primitive weaver had much the same feelir.gs. The weaving process having been invented and mastered, the work would become monotonous. Fibres of different colours had become available, or the possibility of dyeing with roots, leaves, and berries had been discovered, and the weaver would take different colours for her weft merely as a *change*. The result would be *stripes* of colour running across the fabric. Deliberate decoration now became possible, together with a great variety of arrangements.

This was probably the first type of decoration in weaving, and will certainly be the first kind to be attempted by beginners. Experiments may be made in the arrangements of bands of colour, and valuable experience will be gained. Such experiments will lead weavers to see the desirability of preliminary planning. It takes a long time to weave, and to undo the work done is very tiresome. Experiments may therefore be tried by means of coloured paper, by painting in water colour, or by the use of coloured crayons. This latter method is much handier and requires no preparation in the arrangement of bands of different colours, of different widths, and at varying distances apart. The wide range of coloured papers with gummed backs provides an excellent material for this early design. This paper should be cut into strips and applied to tinted paper of the same colour as the groundwork of the material to be woven. If water colours are used, this experiment in making decoration for weaving provides an excellent motive for practice in the control of brush and paint and in the laying on of flat washes. It must, of course, be understood that in ordinary weaving these stripes will never be pure in colour, since the warp will show through.

Having experienced the pleasing effects which resulted from stripes running *across* the fabric, the weaver would probably now conceive the desire to produce stripes down the *length* of material. The ability to produce these indicates a great intellectual advance, because this effect had to be planned in advance and the different colours introduced into the warp. These stripes having been successfully produced, the discovery of plaid patterns comes as a happy accident. The warp has a purposeful variation, the weft is changed for the joy of using different colours, and the surprising result is a plaid! The reader may examine any piece of material with a plaid pattern, and will be interested to trace its construction. Suppose that strips of varying widths of red, blue, and natural raffia are used in the warp and the same colours are woven across. The resulting fabric will have the following patches of colour:

(1) Pure red only in the portions where red weft crosses the red portions of the warp.

(2) Pure blue where blue weft crosses blue warp.

(3) Purple in places where red crosses blue.

(4) Paler, broken red or blue where either of these colours is crossed by the natural weft.

(5) Natural, where natural warp and weft occur at the same place.

The hand-woven raffia fabrics (Rabannes) from Madagascar furnish excellent illustrations of the construction of various plaids.

A vast field of experiment and discovery is now open to the weaver. Raffia will still be the material used, and can be made into table mats, bags, pochettes, book carriers, the backs of blotters, writing cases, and a great variety of useful articles. A word in season with regard to the 'finish' and making up of such articles may not be out of place at this point. Linings, if used, should be suitable in colour and texture. Such materials as sateen, artificial silk, and the like do not suit the texture of the material woven from raffia. Linen is better, or, failing that, casement cloth; and the Madagascar fabric mentioned above makes a very suitable lining material. There should be no attempt to hide the stitchery involved—this may quite well serve the double purpose of *construction* and *decoration*. For fastenings, press studs are too sophisticated, and are incongruous with the primitive appearance of raffia work. More appropriate fastenings are buttons and loops made of plaited raffia (see Fig. 1). The upper flap of a pochette can be slipped under a band of woven or plaited raffia. The handles of bags or book carriers can be made from similar woven or plaited strips. The method of making the woven strip is obvious enough at this stage to need no explanation, but directions for the wide plait may be acceptable, since such a strap may be useful for many purposes. Take any number of strands of raffia (from 4 to 12) according to the width of plait required. Tie each of these on to a pencil, knitting needle, or other thin piece of wood or metal. This should be held by another person, or placed behind two nails driven into the bench (Fig. 10), or it may be tied on to a hook. Now begin with the strand on the extreme left. Weave this under one and over one until it reaches the extreme right and leave it. Take the strand which is now on the left and

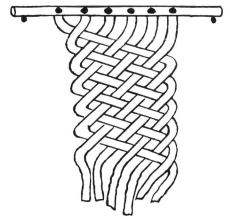

FIG. 10.—Method of making plait.

weave it in turn under one and over one to the right, and so on with each succeeding strand. For the first few rows the process is a little confusing, but once the plait is established it is perfectly easy. When a strand becomes thin and nears its end, place another by its side and weave both together for a few rows. Thus a continuous plait of any length may be produced. In addition to using plaited raffia for handles, etc. it can be stitched together for bags. An excellent example of this is shown in Fig. 1.

Further possibilities for the development of pattern now occur through a variation in the actual weaving process. Hitherto the weft has been threaded regularly under one and over one warp strand. If it is now taken under two and over two a larger check pattern will result. A 'basket pattern' effect will be produced by weaving over three and under one, reversing the process in alternate rows. A 'twill' pattern is produced by weaving over three and under one if each row is started differently so that the 'over three' movement of the weft starts one thread nearer to the left than in the previous row, viz., using a warp having a multiple of four as the total number of its strands.

1st row : (*under one, over three*); repeat (*   *) to end of row.

Return over one, under one, (* over three, under one*); repeat (*   *).

3rd row : under one, over one, under one, (*over three, under one*); repeat.

Return under one, over one, under one, (*over three, under one*); repeat.

The under side of the fabric thus produced shows a reverse of this pattern, the predominant colour on the upper surface becoming the subsidiary one on the under side.

A little experience in weaving this simple twill will lead to the suggestion of several variations of twill patterns, and also of many attractive 'all-over patterns', suggestions for which are given in Fig. 11. The worker will easily devise other simple patterns, but should realise that the fabric thus made will be loose in texture. In no case should a pattern be used which involves weaving under or over more than five strands at a time, as this would make the material too loose to be of any practical use. (See Figs. 11, 12 and 14 for examples of all-over patterns.)

Other interesting patterns may be produced by alternating two colours in warp threads of one colour followed by one of another, and then weaving with one of these colours or a different one. It will be obvious that the colours of the

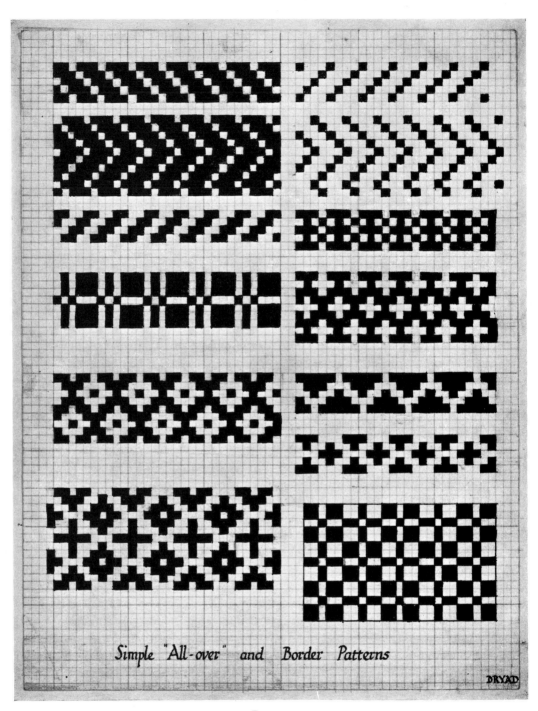

Simple "All-over" and Border Patterns

DRYAD

FIG. 11.

14

FIG. 12.—ALL-OVER PATTERNS. SMALL ARTICLES MADE WITH WOOL WOVEN ON CARDBOARD FRAMES.

weft must not be very frequently changed at this stage owing to the difficulty of keeping the work neat. The scarf illustrated (Fig. 62) is produced as follows: Warp black and white alternately 12 threads; then white and black alternately 12 threads; then black and white alternately 12 threads; and so on according to the width required. Weave 12 rows with black; 12 with white; and 12 with alternate rows of black and white (using two shuttles). Continue weaving in this order when an interesting check pattern will result.

FIG. 13.—SAMPLER SHOWING VARIETY OF WOVEN PATTERNS USING NEEDLE OR SHUTTLE ONLY.

15

FIG. 14.—ALL-OVER PATTERNS. EXPERIMENTS WITH WOOL ON CARDBOARD.

It may be a saving of time for such experimental work in pattern weaving to be done with paper, as suggested in Chapter II. Such paper material for weaving can still be purchased from educational supply firms—a relic of the old 'Kindergarten Occupations', but whereas it then provided only mechanical activity, it can now be used intelligently and for a definite purpose. After a little practice in making patterns in paper, weavers will be able to use squared paper for this purpose (as in Fig. 11), and so effect a great saving of time.

The subject of pattern cannot be left without mentioning the possibility of 'warp' patterns, although the opportunity to use these will not come until later, when the weaver has appliances which will enable her to use a warp of as many as 30 threads to the inch. If the reader cares to experiment she may fix up a simple sample warp on cardboard, as pictured in Fig. 15, but the

16

weaving of long pieces of work would be tiresome with such modest equipment as is at present available. Some suggestions are shown in Fig. 16.

An excellent loom on which to make braids, etc., with warp patterns is the Scottish Inkle Loom described later in Chapter VI.

In this kind of weaving the warp threads are so close that the weft does not show at all in the finished work, its function being only structural, i.e., to hold down the interchanged warp threads and form them into a fabric. These warp patterns are apt to be very surprising to the beginner, but are easily understood. If a warp is made of alternate threads of red and green closely packed, i.e., 32 or more to the inch, and this is woven in the ordinary way, what happens is this :

The first pass of the weft picking up alternate strands picks up all the red ones, and since the weft does not show, this makes a line of red across the work. The next row of weaving picks up all the green, with the result that from a warp with vertical stripes of red and green we produce a braid having *horizontal* stripes in those colours. If vertical bands of colour are required, two, four, or more strands of that colour must be adjacent in the warp, and it should be noted that these will not result in straight lines, but in slightly zigzag continuous bands of colour, since they are formed by picking up adjacent threads of the same colour in successive passes of the weft.

FIG. 15.—WARP PATTERNS.

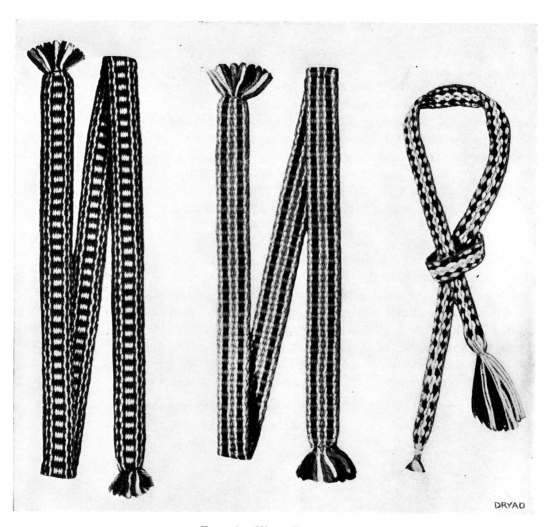

Fig. 16.—Warp Patterns.

18

II. Colour

The beauty of hand-woven fabric depends, not only on texture and pattern, but even to a greater extent on colour, and before the weaver proceeds much further with the technique of weaving, it would be well to give some attention to this subject.

Many fortunate weavers will have the guidance of natural taste in this direction—but may be happy to have their ideas justified by the enunciation of some guiding principles; and to others who doubt their own ability, some general suggestions will undoubtedly be welcome.

All readers are familiar with the old classification of colours into *Primary* (Red, Blue, Yellow) and *Secondary* (Orange, Green, Purple). A more useful guide is to use the arrangement of colours in the spectrum. These are: Violet, Indigo, Blue, Green, Yellow, Orange, Red. These should be arranged in the above order with coloured paper to form a circle. Roughly speaking, it may be said that within this circle the adjacent colours will harmonise with each other, and that the approximately opposite pairs give the best contrasts. In arranging a colour scheme a little contrast is often valuable, but it must be used sparingly, with due regard to proportion.

A good general rule is: 'much of one colour with very little of its contrast'. At the moment of writing the author visualises a room decorated and furnished in a pleasant scheme of pink-mauve. It is restful but cries out for a touch of relief and must one day be given a cushion or vase in perhaps a light bright green.

Material with equal amounts of red and green would be ugly, whereas a green article with a narrow edge or tiny trimming of red, or vice-versa, would be quite pleasing. A fabric made with a red warp and green weft would again be quite ugly, and the same is true of all opposite or widely contrasting colours. On the other hand, a warp and weft of adjacent colours would give a fabric of far more interest than if warp and weft were the same in either one of the colours.

Now to return to the colour circle. If this were painted in water colour, allowing the damp colours to run into each other, a further range of intermediate colours would result, from which similar but more varied and interesting colour harmonies might be arranged.

Again, if all the colours were darkened in differing degrees by the addition of black, or thinned, thus allowing more of the white paper to show through, an even greater variety of intermediate colours would result. As the mixtures get further removed from the primary, secondary and tertiary colours the results would tend to those frequently termed pastel colours; delicate greys, which for closer distinction could be termed greenish grey, blueish grey, purplish grey, etc., according to the basic colour.

To all these ranges the following general principle applies:

Harmonise by using (*a*) Adjacent colours

(*b*) Lighter or darker forms of the same colour

(*c*) Contrasting colours in small quantities

(*d*) A combination of *a*, *b*, and *c*

In dealing with the subject of colour it is impossible to overstress the value of the *Neutrals*.

Grey, in its various gradations from white to black, is a most valuable neutralising agent and may with advantage be largely used. The soft greys of natural Shetland wool form an excellent background for most colour schemes and the adult weaver is advised to plan colour schemes on a neutral ground instead of using colours of the desired range throughout.

Pure black and pure white 'go' with pure bright colours—the best being red, and following that perhaps emerald green and bright yellow. None will deny the freshness of such combinations, but unless the bright freshness is specifically desired, the softer colours are more pleasing. Though pure black and white are difficult to handle, the same is not true of the 'nearly black' and 'not quite white'—perhaps 'dark brown' and 'off white'. The natural colours of sheep's wool—by no means black—white unbleached, and natural grey, will form some of the most valuable material for the discriminating weaver, for whom they may serve as backgrounds, as softening lines between masses of colour or as quiet and pleasing schemes in themselves.

The beautiful blankets woven by North American Indians make generous use of these colours, often in combination with a 'madder' red giving the happiest of results.

In using cottons, linens, etc., unless pure white is actually needed for a special purpose, the unbleached fibres are likely to produce more interesting fabrics in themselves, and also to provide better background for other colours.

A really valuable experience for the weaver in search of good colour arrangements would be to set up a warp in fine wool with fourteen or more threads to the inch, and consisting of two inches of each of the spectrum colours, also of black, white, grey, and perhaps other neutrals such as beige and brown, and then to weave across with each of the warp colours in turn.

Some illuminating effects would result and would serve as useful reference for future work.

III. Texture

There is a danger that the amateur weaver may be so fascinated by the interest of colour schemes or intrigued by the intricacies of pattern drafting that she may entirely overlook the beauty and interest of texture alone. Yet this offers so many possibilities of variety and individual expression and so many problems of *fitness for purpose* that it may well occupy the whole attention of even skilled weavers. It should certainly be the object of study and experiment by all beginners.

FIG. 17.—A gay cushion on a white mercerised cotton warp with an assortment of bright oddments for weft—wool, cotton and strips of rag.

Is the woven fabric intended to make a scarf, a cushion square handbag, floor rug, car rug, dress or coat material, curtains, towel, or table napkin? In every case the weaver must consider not only the number of threads to the inch, but the type of yarn to be used and the kind of fleece and spinning technique necessary to produce this. For instance, a scarf to be 'cosy' should be light in weight and loosely woven. The wool should be preferably hand-spun—more tightly spun for warp than weft. If hand-spun warp is not available, single-ply machine-spun wool can be used, with loosely hand-spun weft. Material for a suit needs to be more closely woven from more tightly spun yarn, so that it will not stretch and sag in wear.

Again, compare the desirable qualities in car rugs and floor rugs respectively. The former are charming and practical if loosely woven in coarse hand-spun wool, but a floor rug must be tough and not easily kicked about. Such a rug may be woven on a cotton string warp with about six threads to the inch,

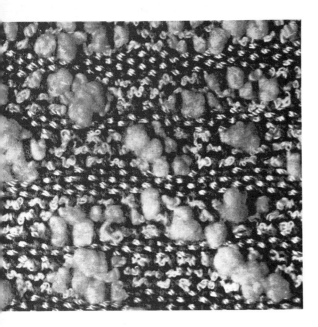

FIG. 18.—EXPERIMENTS WITH TEXTURE MADE BY BOYS OF HABERDASHERS' ASKE'S SCHOOL, HAMPSTEAD.

1. Warp : wool.
   Weft : wool, cotton gimp and rayon.

2. Warp : wool.
   Weft : wool, cotton gimp and black plastic strips.

3. Warp : wool.
   Weft : wool, crinkle cotton, cotton gimp and plastic strips.

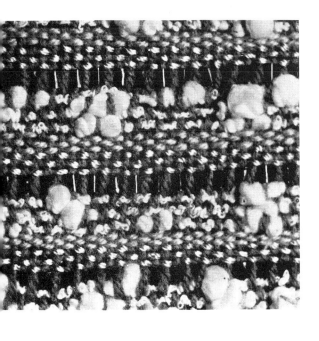

FIG. 18 (CONTD.).

4. Warp : wool.
   Weft : wool, crinkle cotton, rayon and plastic strips.

5. Warp : **yellow wool.**
   Weft : **cream rayon,** brown wool **and** bronze tinsel.

6. Warp : wool.
   Weft : wool, etc. Several rows of wool inserted in the same shed to lend interest to the texture.

FIG. 19.—Two cushions woven on a simple two-way loom, showing the introduction of thick slub cotton, on a wool warp, to give variety in texture.

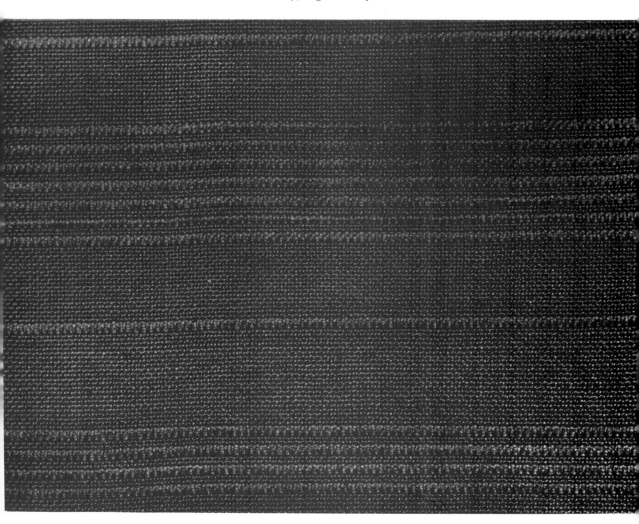

FIG. 20.—Texture produced by inserting several rows of weft in the same shed, at intervals : beige mercerised warp ; green mercerised weft. Dentage 28 (2 threads per dent).

24

with a tightly packed weft of thick hand-spun or single-ply rug wool, or, alternatively, as on the Inkle loom, with a thick closely-packed warp and thin sparse weft. A dress material should be finer and more closely woven than that required, for instance, to make a light summer coat. For table napkins and towels, linen and cotton threads will be used, with 28 or 32 threads to the inch, and these demand mainly regular uniform texture.

The essential texture of curtain material is that it should 'drape' or 'hang' well. A lightly spun weft, with a 'tougher' warp and weaving not too close is suggested. When the demands of function have been satisfied there still remains the possibility of decoration, even in a self-colour scheme, by means of variation in texture. Thicker materials may be used, giving bands, checks and plaids in raised pattern. A most attractive summer handbag was woven from white knitting cotton and thicker, loosely spun white cotton used for making raised bands.

Weft threads may often be used in bunches of three or four, giving a pleasing variation. An interesting example of this is seen in Fig. 22. The woven material would be most suitable for a light shawl or blanket. Fig. 20 shows a similar idea used for curtain material. This was woven with green mercerised cotton weft on a beige mercerised cotton warp—giving an interesting shot effect to the fabric. Odd lengths of thicker yarn may be inserted at intervals in the warp or in both warp and weft, thus giving a periodic thickening to the fabric.

A warp thicker than the weft gives a longitudinal ribbed effect, while a thicker weft has the opposite result.

Interesting effects are produced by mixing different yarns—wool, silk, gimp, chenille, slub, cotton and linen in the same fabric. Metal threads and even cellophane have been used successfully for decoration. Some interesting experiments with these materials are shown in Fig. 18 and in the three cushions, Figs. 17 and 19. Descriptions of these materials are given in Chapter XVI on 'Materials for Use'.

For practical purposes, however, the weaver should assure herself that the fibres used will wear, and clean or wash together, otherwise the article will be short-lived.

Experiment on the lines indicated will be both amusing and profitable, but the ultimate aim of the weaver must be to produce *a texture appropriate to the purpose the material is intended to serve.*

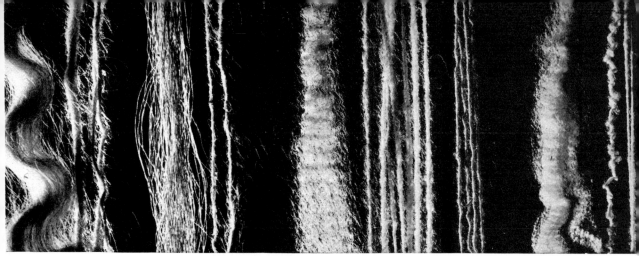

FIG. 21

FIG. 22

Texture has for some years been a main study of the weavers at Howell's School, Denbigh. Fig. 21 indicates something of their range of raw material, various fleece and the yarns into which they spin it, and Fig. 22 shows the various types of cloth produced by them as a result of this basic interest in texture.

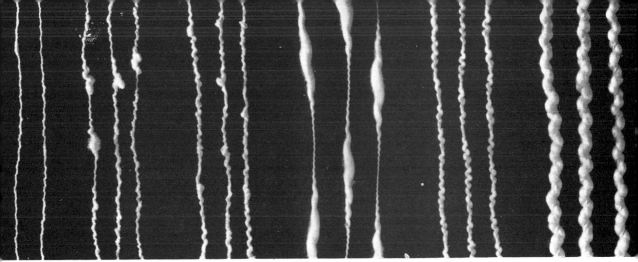

FIG. 23

FIG. 24

Three travelling rugs woven from hand-spun wool by pupils of Howell's School, Denbigh. Although the same article has been made by several pupils, the results differ widely. Each is the expression of individual ideas and taste, and the difference is seen in colour, pattern, and above all, in texture. Fig. 23 shows a variety of fancy cottons, described in Chapter XVI, Materials for Use.

FIG. 25.—Wool spun with spindle and woven by twelve-year-old boy from Haberdashers' Aske's School, Hampstead.

Footnote for Teachers

It seemed necessary to introduce the subject of colour at this stage, since children need early education in this direction, and no ugly work should be produced. It was not practicable, however, to distribute notes on colour throughout the book, so practically the whole range of the subject has been at least indicated in this chapter.

It will be obvious that children must be introduced gradually to the various phases. Generally speaking, the simple spectrum colours will provide ample material for experiment and choice in the Infant School, and the various colours made by blending these for the lower classes of the Junior School. In the Senior School pupils should have access to a greater variety of coloured weaving materials such as wools, cottons, linens, etc. It will be found that by twisting together (with the fingers) two or more threads of carefully chosen colours, many happy combinations will result. To get the desired effect the threads should be well twisted.

A more satisfactory method than using the fingers would be to use a bobbin winder or spindle to produce a twisted thread. This should give a more accurate conception of the colour likely to result in the woven fabric but the twisted thread should include at least one of the warp threads.

Teachers may, without actually prescribing rules for colour selection, lead their pupils to produce tasteful work by allowing a restricted choice of materials, and by tactfully leading children to compare the results of different colour combinations before embarking on a piece of work. The value of the influence of examples of good craftsmanship and of pictures should not be overlooked, and the school furnishing and decoration should exert an unconscious influence for good.

The pupils in at least one school of the writers' acquaintance produce beautiful colour schemes in weaving through a study of nature. The reader will easily imagine the colour selection inspired by a study of beech trees in autumn, a bunch of delphiniums, a sunset sky, or the twilight colours of woods and mountains. It is interesting to note that not only with regard to the choice of colours but also in the matter of their respective proportions was the guidance of nature sound. Some perfectly balanced colour schemes were produced from a study of the colours of moths and butterflies. It may be well worth while to experiment in sending the pupils to nature for inspiration for their colour schemes.

Finally, it seems desirable to emphasise once more the value of wool in its natural colours, and of the vegetable dyes. When the latter are used it is much more difficult to produce ugly colour combinations than is the case with commercial dyestuffs.

CHAPTER IV

By-ways

IN previous chapters the historical sequence in the development of the weaver's craft has been more or less closely followed. It is convenient here to make a slight detour for the sake of describing some miscellaneous forms of weaving which may be acceptable to the worker at this stage:

1. *Various Forms of Weaving with Raffia, Wool, or Stiff Paper on Cardboard.*

(*a*) Several useful articles, such as small bags, handkerchief sachets and book carriers, can be made all in a piece, instead of by means of sewing up a flat piece of fabric, if both sides of the piece of cardboard are used. To make a bag, use the cardboard pierced with holes as described in Chapter II. In warping remember that the top of the bag must be left open and the bottom closed. The warp is therefore carried at the top *through the holes and back*, but at the bottom it is taken through the holes, and up to the top, where it is taken again *through and back* (Fig. 26a).

The course of the warp which has been tied through hole No. 1 is: down to 1 *b*, through, up the back of cardboard to 1, through 1 to the front, back through 2 down the back to 2 *b*, up the front to 2, through to the back, return through 3, down the front to 3 *b*, and so on.

As there must be an odd number of threads to carry the weaving continuously round two sides of the cardboard, an extra warp strand must be added on one side of the card. This can be done by piercing an extra hole, or taking two warp strands through the last hole. See that the warp threads are quite close to the edges of the boards, or there will be a loose patch down the sides of the bag. The weaving can now be started. Instead of going backwards and forwards on one side of the cardboard the weft is taken continuously across the front, round the back, round to the front, and so on.

An alternative method is to warp from side to side of the cardboard (Fig. 26b).[1] The weaving then starts at the top (A), goes *round* the cardboard at the bottom (B) up to A, where it returns to B, round B and up to A, where it returns. In this case care must be exercised not to pull the weft too tightly, or the opening at the top of the bag will be pulled out of the straight. The difference in result of the two methods is that in the first, stripes made by changing the weft colour will go *across* the bag, whilst in the second method

---

[1]It will be obvious, from a glance at the diagrams, that holes in the cardboard could be dispensed with at the bottom of Fig. 26a and at both sides in Fig. 26b, the warp being simply carried round the cardboard. But for an inexperienced weaver it is easier to have the warp kept in place by means of the holes. The cardboard is afterwards torn away along the lines of the holes, and the remainder removed from between the weaving.

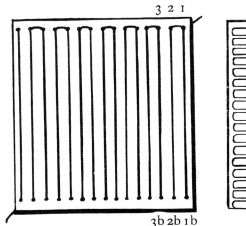

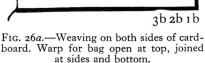

FIG. 26a.—Weaving on both sides of cardboard. Warp for bag open at top, joined
at sides and bottom.

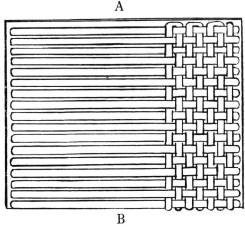

FIG. 26b.—Weaving on both sides of cardboard.
Bag opening at A.

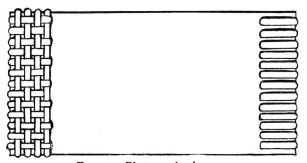

FIG. 27.—Blotter or book cover.

such stripes will go down the bag. Handles should be added to make a bag,
or a button and loop for a handkerchief sachet. To make a book carrier or
blotter cover, the warp should be put on both sides of the board at the portions
into which the book cover slips, and on one side only in the other portions
(Figs. 26b and 27). Wide-plaited or woven straps should be added, which
should preferably go all round the carrier.

(b) *Circular Weaving*.—Circular raffia mats are useful as tea-pot stands,
lunch mats, and for placing under flower vases which are sometimes slightly
porous and might mark the tops of tables. These mats may be made in two
ways : (1) By weaving on both sides of the cardboard foundation, leaving this
inside, and (2) by weaving on one side only, the cardboard being removed
when this is finished (Figs. 28a and 28b).

For the first mat take a circular piece of cardboard of 5 to 8 inches in diameter, according to the purpose for which it is intended. In the centre cut a

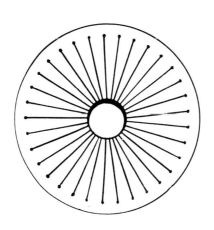

FIG. 28a.—Circular weaving on both sides of cardboard.

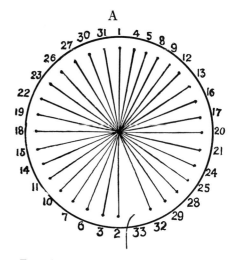

FIG. 28b.—Circular mat woven on one side of cardboard only.

circular hole 1 inch in diameter. Draw a circle ¼ inch from the outer edge, and on this mark with compasses or dividers dots at a distance of approximately ½ inch apart, making an odd number. Thread the warp through the board at one of these points, and tie it temporarily round the edge of the board. Now take it down to the centre hole, through this, up the back through the next point, down the front, through centre, and so on until the warp is completed. Tie the end round the edge of the board. Start weaving as near the centre as possible, leaving an end to be threaded into the work when finished; when one row of weaving has been done pull the weft tightly, and with the needle press it in close to the centre hole. Continue weaving until one side is finished, and then work the other side. The weft may be varied so as to produce bands of colour, and interest is added by the fact that, the warp being closely packed near the centre, its colour predominates here, and gradually disappears towards the circumference, where it is more widely spaced and is covered by the weft. The knots at the beginning and end of the warp are untied, and the ends darned neatly into the fabric. The superfluous cardboard is cut away at the edge, which may be finished by a narrow plait or twisted cord.

The second type of mat is a little more difficult. Here the warp is apparently stretched from one point on the circumference to a point diametrically opposite, but as it is necessary to have an odd number of strands, it is obvious that this simple mathematical arrangement will not suffice. Perhaps the simplest method of arranging the warp is as follows: divide the circumference into eight equal parts (this is most easily done by folding a paper of the required size, placing this on the card, and marking the ends of the folds with a pencil on the card). Now divide each eighth into four equal parts, except the top right-hand section, which is divided into five. Mark the top A, as in Fig. 28b. Now if the warping follows the arrangement of the numbers in the diagram, it is obvious that the strand coming out at 33 must go to the centre. Here it is wrapped round the other warp strands, and may be used to start the weaving.

These circular mats may be made into very attractive hand-bags if two of them are joined for three-quarters of their circumference by means of a strip of woven raffia about 1 inch wide, which adds to the capacity of the bag and is continued to form a handle (see Fig. 30). The beret is made as follows: on a sheet of cardboard make a circle of the required size to fit a child's head, and outside this a concentric circle the size of the finished hat. Divide the circle into six equal parts (by marking off the radius on circumference) and then into twelve. Counting point A (Fig. 29) as the first, mark on the first section of the circumference five equidistant points, and in all other sections six points, always counting the dividing point as the first. Thread warp from front to back at point x—leaving the end loose at front, come to the front at a, up to A, across the back to B up to b, through and back to c down to C, across the back to D down to d, and so on, until the last end finishes at x, where it can be tied to the starting end, or used as weft. The method of weaving needs no description. A development of this circular weaving leads to the attractive shell-shaped bag and tea and egg cosies illustrated in Figs. 30 and 31. The cardboard foundations for these may be bought ready-made, but are perfectly easy to make. The 'corner-stone' of their construction is a pair of brass or bone curtain rings about $\frac{1}{2}$ inch in diameter. They are fastened one on either side in the centre of a piece of cardboard an inch from the upper edge, by stitching the upper part of the rings through the cardboard (Fig. 32). The shape may be varied, and is most easily obtained by folding a piece of paper length-wise and cutting the required curve. This is opened out, placed on the cardboard, and its outline marked. Holes are pierced about $\frac{3}{8}$ inch apart along this line. The warp is tied through the ring on the front of the board, carried through the first hole on the

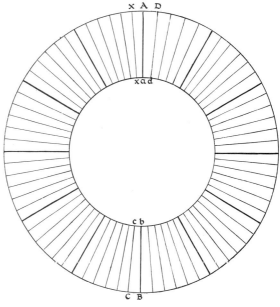

FIG. 29.—Threading up a warp for beret.

33

Fig. 30.—Circular Weaving.

FIG. 31.—Set of Egg Cosies with case woven in one piece as described in this chapter.
Colour—a harmony of yellows.

right across the back of board and through the ring on that side, back to
the next hole, across the front to the ring, and so on. When a few strands
have been warped on the right-hand side a similar number should be put on
the left to prevent the ring being pulled from the centre. The warp must not
be too tightly stretched, as it will be taken up by the great number of weft
strands which must be inserted. The weaving is started as for the circular mats,
as near as possible to the centre. The first weft strand is then pulled tightly to
draw it into the ring, and is pushed up with a needle. The weaving proceeds as
usual, care being taken not to spoil the straight lines at the top of the work by
pulling the weft too tightly. An interesting gradation of colours occurs, because
the warp colour predominates near the ring and is gradually covered by the
weft; and pleasant results may be produced by varying the colours in warp and
weft. When both surfaces have been woven the cardboard is removed, and the
ring should be covered by means of 'blanket-stitching' with raffia, and if for a
bag, a handle should be provided in the form of a woven or plaited strip stitched

through the rings. Wooden beads may, with advantage, be stitched on at the points where the warp apparently terminates round the edge of the bag.

The slippers (Fig. 32) arc produced by a combination of straight and circular weaving. To plan these, obtain a pair of fleecy-lined soles of the required size. Then make, on cardboard, a sketch similar to that in Fig. 32, but see that the outer edge of the pattern is slightly larger than the outer edge of the slipper soles to allow for a little fullness at the toes. The warp threads should be $\frac{1}{4}$ inch apart. For the straight part of the slipper they go always 'through and

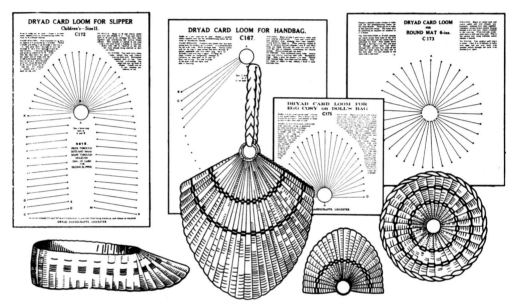

Fig. 32.—Adaptations of the cardboard foundation to give variety of shapes.

back', but for the curved portion they go through a hole to the front, across, and through ring, back across the front to the next hole, through and back to the front, and so on. The weaving starts at D, proceeds up this inner edge, round the ring, down to the lower edge on the opposite side, then returns by the same route to D, and so on until the whole surface is covered. A warm lining is then stitched to the woven fabric. The back seam is joined, the woven top is stitched to the sole, and the upper edge of slipper finished with a neat plait.

2. Lavender 'Bottles' (Figs. 33a, b, c)

These provide an attractive kind of weaving for country dwellers when the lavender is in flower. They are quickly made and form dainty gifts, as they are acceptable for use in the linen drawer. The lavender stalks form the warp, and the weft should be *bébé* ribbon. An odd number of lavender spikes should be

36

used (say 19 or 21). These are tied together with one end of the weft just below
the flower heads. The bunch is then held with the heads downwards, and the
stalks are sharply bent over the tie till they form a sort of 'cage' round the
flower heads. The weft is now taken under and over these stalks until the
flower heads are completely enclosed. It is now wrapped round and round
the stalks for a few inches, and finished with a bow, which must be stitched
securely in position.

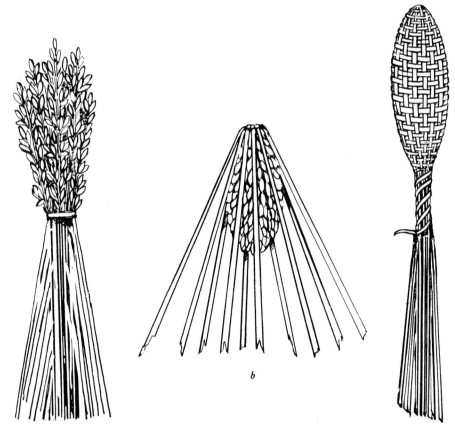

a   FIGS. 33*a*, *b*, and *c*.—Weaving of Lavender Bottles.   *c*

3. *Table Mats, Tea-pot Stands, etc., made from Straws* (Fig. 34)

These useful articles may be made in colours to match the table ware, and as
they can be washed with soap and water they are very durable. They provide
an opportunity to use many of the simple patterns devised when experimenting
with paper work (Chapter III).

The straws are of the same kind as those served with lemonade, and may be
bought in a variety of colours, together with a straw plait for edging the mats.

DRYAD

FIG. 34.—STRAW MATS.

The straws are split by inserting a small penknife at one end and running it up the straw. They are then opened out by drawing the penknife up the length of the straw whilst holding the lower end firmly in the left hand. Cardboard foundations are cut to the required size and shape (preferably square or rectangular at first, though the weaver will soon learn to manage other shapes). The 'warp' straws are then stitched along the upper edge of the cardboard, and the weft straws are woven across until the surface is covered, when the edges are stitched to keep them in place. The other side is covered in the same way. The edges are then trimmed and finished by sewing a narrow straw plait on each side. Half straws may be used for smaller patterns.

4. *Weaving with Felt Remnants*

Bedside strips, door mats, bungalow mats, and hearth rugs may be cheaply made by using felt remnants and offcuts. The idea of this form of weaving as a useful hobby was suggested by a recollection of the mats woven in squares of red and black, or red and grey, seen during childhood in country cottages. They were usually purchased from gipsy pedlars. The remnants are supplied in assorted colours, and may be curved strips cut from the outer edges of the brims of felt hats. An old picture frame forms the loom, or a clothes

38

FIG. 35.—RUG WOVEN FROM FELT REMNANTS.

FIG. 36.—SHOPPING BAG AND POCHETTES. SIMPLE WEAVING IN BRAIDS.
THE BAG WAS WOVEN OVER A CARDBOARD BOX.

39

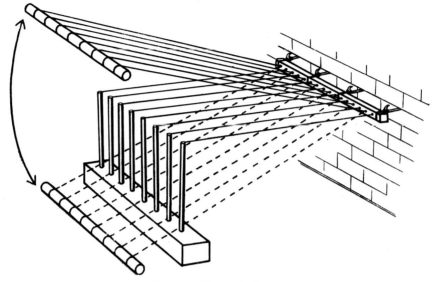

FIG. 37.—Scout Mat Loom.

horse or a deck chair would serve, the warp strands being fixed with tacks to the upper and lower bars. The strips must first be straightened by stretching, and will stretch more easily if slightly warmed. They must then be cut into strips of uniform width. Pieces which are not long enough should be neatly stitched together. The actual weaving needs no explanation at this stage. Very pleasing results are possible if the colours are well chosen (see Fig. 35). All-over check patterns, or plain centres with broken stripes round the edges, and a variety of plaids may easily be produced. When the weaving is finished it will be necessary to stitch round the edges to keep it in place. The ends of warp and weft strands may be left free beyond this stitching to form a fringe, or they may be turned in and fastened down.

Another useful loom for school purposes is an adaptation of a Scout Mat Loom (Fig. 37). This has been improvised at the request of a teacher of physical training, to meet the need for coarse mats to be used for some of the exercises carried out in the playground. Junior scholars, especially boys, enjoy this work, and the cost of such mats is negligible. The work may be done out of doors if space is a difficulty in the schoolroom. A piece of wood 2 feet 3 inches long and about 2 inches square section is tied to four hooks driven into a wall at a height of about 2 feet. On this the warp threads, sixteen in number, and consisting of coarse string used double, are tied at regular intervals. For the other end of the loom a length of wood is required, 2 feet 3 inches long, of 4-inch square section (or even larger) into which eight strong stakes, square or round, 2 feet high and of about $1\frac{1}{2}$ inches section, are firmly fixed. This is placed at the required distance from the wall, and must be fixed in position with tent pegs (or with angle-irons and screws if indoors). The alternate warp strands are now firmly attached to the tops of these stakes. The others are tied on to a broom handle placed behind the pegs, care being taken that they are in their proper position, alternating with the fixed threads. Two workers are necessary. The weft may be of natural rush, straw, or any other cheap and coarse material. One worker raises the broom handle shoulder high, thus raising alternate warp strands, and the other inserts the weft and packs it tightly. The broom handle is now lowered to the floor, taking down the same set of strands, and thus making the second shed. The packing must be vigorously done. The mat is finished off by tying the warp threads together in pairs.

FINGER WEAVING

The weaver who has become interested in the problem of devices for producing the shed in weaving may like to experiment with a simple method which dispenses with equipment. It occupies two weavers and uses only eight warp threads, which are drawn tightly together to produce a narrow braid. Children find this an interesting activity, as the braids grow very quickly.

The fingers of one weaver form the loom, while the other person passes the shuttle. A braid with horizontal stripes of red and blue is made as follows. Four red threads are tied with slip knots one to each finger of the hand, and four blue ones in the same way on the other hand. The other ends of the threads are tied together and attached to a string which is tied round the waist of the other weaver. The first weaver now crosses the fingers of the two hands, thus making a shed through which the shuttle is passed by the weaver. The fingers are then uncrossed and another pass of the shuttle is made. The two movements are repeated and a braid is very quickly produced.

The weaver who has studied 'warp patterns', Chapter III, will realise that vertical stripes may also be produced in this way.

CHAPTER V

New Materials

"She seeketh wool and flax, and worketh willingly with her hands."—Prov. xxxi. 13.

THE arrangement of this book has been based on the assumption that the practice of the art of weaving preceded the discovery of spinning—an assumption which must be well founded, since it was possible to weave with vegetable fibres in their natural state. At what period of history the art of spinning was discovered it is not possible to say, but it was certainly very early, because spun threads and spinning instruments are found amongst the earliest relics of primitive man. Pliny ascribes the invention of weaving, which must undoubtedly have included spinning, to the Egyptians, and the mummy cloths and bandages found in ancient Egyptian tombs are woven from finely spun flaxen threads, as also are the fragments of fabric from the lake-dwellings of Switzerland which may be seen in the British Museum. References to the arts of spinning and weaving, and to 'fine linen', are frequent in the Old Testament.

The reader may imagine the satisfaction of some early experimenter who discovered that a continuous thread might be made from short vegetable fibres or from the wool or hair of animals by twisting it between the fingers.[1] Still more pleasing would be the subsequent discovery that a stone or other weight attached to a thread, twisted, and allowed to fall, would considerably hasten the twisting process. Many primitive peoples of today practise spinning by just such simple methods. The spindle, which was the only equipment used for spinning until the invention of the spinning-wheel in the sixteenth century, represents only a slight advance on this.

The first wool weaving the learner will undertake will be done on cardboard foundations as described in Chapter II for raffia work. Similar articles will be made, but the weaving will be finer. For the purpose of this early work, and perhaps for the bulk of the wool weaving, the material used will be bought ready prepared (machine spun and dyed with commercial dyes), but our pupils may well, at this stage, make experiments in the use of the spindle, and should endeavour to spin by this means enough *weft* for a very small article (the *warp* needs a stronger fibre than can be produced by the amateur). Before the

---

[1] A young New Zealand farmer was interested to find a spinning-wheel in the writer's home. He asked to be taught to spin, and also to be allowed to make working drawings of the wheel, as he wished to make one for his mother on his return to New Zealand. She had been anxious to use the wool from their own sheep, and had been patiently drawing out the fleece and twisting it in her fingers inch by inch. She had actually sent to her relatives in England a knitted shawl, the wool for which she had spun by this laborious process. It is interesting to speculate as to how long it would have taken this twentieth-century worker to devise for herself a method used by all primitive peoples.

method of doing this is described it will be necessary to give some account of the preparation of the wool prior to this stage. (Flax, cotton, and silk are not introduced until a later stage in this volume, as the amateur will weave mainly with wool, but children who have become interested in the industrial arts may like to know something about the preparation of these other fibres, and the teacher should be prepared to satisfy this desire. For this purpose books of reference are mentioned in the Bibliography. Children will also, at this stage, watch with increased interest the activities of the spider, and might be encouraged to keep silkworms.)

The sheep are usually washed a few days before the shearing, but the fleece is still greasy, and probably holds bits of straw and other foreign material, and for this reason in the manufacturing process the wool is first *scoured* (i.e. washed several times in warm soapy water and well rinsed). This removes all natural grease, and to facilitate spinning the wool must then be sprinkled with olive oil. The amateur often prefers to spin before scouring the wool, as this natural grease holds the fibres together and makes the process easier.

The wool is not unpleasant to handle; in fact, its natural grease has a good effect on the skin of the hands. Before it

FIG. 38.—Home-made spindle.

can be spun the wool must first be 'teased' with the fingers, pulling the wool out from its matted state and removing particles of twig, leaves, etc., and afterwards 'carded', though some workers who spin 'in the grease' find that the former process suffices.

For carding, a pair of 'cards' is needed, i.e. two flat pieces of wood with handles (Figs. 39a, b, c). The wood is covered on one side with leather, into which are inserted over the whole surface bent wires turning towards the handle. The worker sits down, and takes one card in the left hand, placing it on her lap with the wires uppermost and the handle pointing to the left. On this she places a small portion of fleece. Now, with the other card in the right hand, the handle pointing to the right, she draws this several times across the left (Fig. 39a) until almost all the wool is on the right-hand card. This is returned to the left by turning the left-hand card and pointing both handles towards the worker, then pushing the right-hand card across the left (Fig. 39b). This process is repeated several times, and then the wool which is on the left-hand card is removed by placing the cards as in Fig. 39c, and scraping the left-hand card down across the edge of the right. The wool is now lifted, by drawing the left-hand card lightly upwards, and then dropped on to the back

43

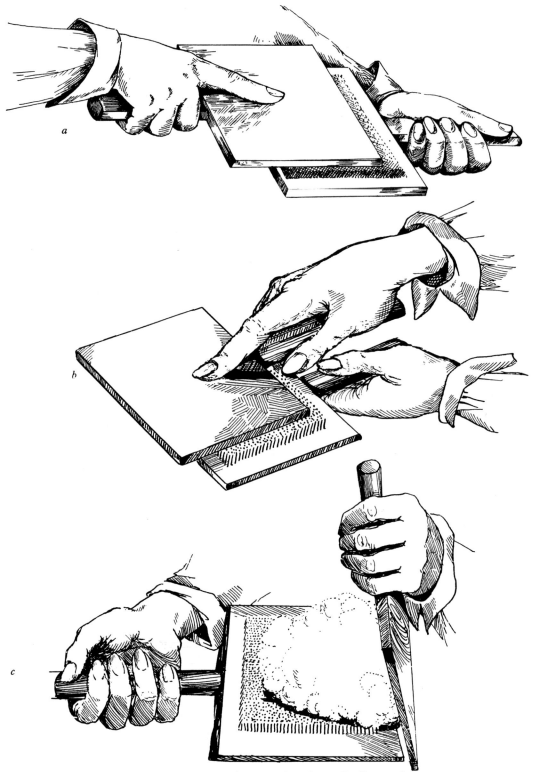

FIGS. 39a, b, and c.—Carding wool.

FIG. 40.—Spinning.

of the right-hand card, where it is rolled between the two card backs into a neat roll, or 'rolag'.

The spindle with which the first spinning will be done, and which is similar to the ones used from the earliest times until the sixteenth century, consists of a thin round piece of hardwood about 12 inches long with a hook at the top and a whorl of hardwood a few inches from the bottom. The fleece is drawn out from the 'rolag', and twisted with the fingers to the desired thickness. When a length of about 2 feet has been sufficiently twisted, tie it round the pillar of the spindle, then carry it round the end of the spindle below the whorl, and loop the thread round the hook at the top with a half hitch (see Fig. 41). To do this, have the wool on the right-hand side of the spindle. Place the forefinger of the right hand behind the thread, then twist the finger backwards over it, thus forming a loop which is slipped on to the hook. Having drawn out a length of fibre from the 'rolag', give the spindle a sharp outward twist and let it fall, meanwhile holding the wool near the 'rolag' with the right fingers and thumb. When the wool is well twisted, rest the spindle, draw out more fibres, relax the hold of the right hand, and the twist will run into the drawn-out fibre. Keep a firm hold with the left hand to prevent the twist extending into the 'rolag'. Repeat this process until the spun yarn is too long for further spinning, then wind this on to the

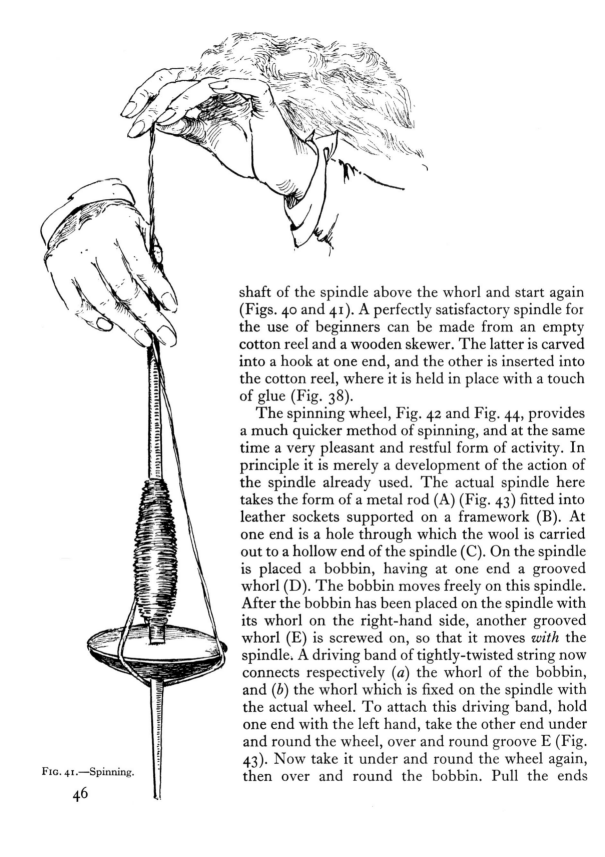

shaft of the spindle above the whorl and start again (Figs. 40 and 41). A perfectly satisfactory spindle for the use of beginners can be made from an empty cotton reel and a wooden skewer. The latter is carved into a hook at one end, and the other is inserted into the cotton reel, where it is held in place with a touch of glue (Fig. 38).

The spinning wheel, Fig. 42 and Fig. 44, provides a much quicker method of spinning, and at the same time a very pleasant and restful form of activity. In principle it is merely a development of the action of the spindle already used. The actual spindle here takes the form of a metal rod (A) (Fig. 43) fitted into leather sockets supported on a framework (B). At one end is a hole through which the wool is carried out to a hollow end of the spindle (C). On the spindle is placed a bobbin, having at one end a grooved whorl (D). The bobbin moves freely on this spindle. After the bobbin has been placed on the spindle with its whorl on the right-hand side, another grooved whorl (E) is screwed on, so that it moves *with* the spindle. A driving band of tightly-twisted string now connects respectively (*a*) the whorl of the bobbin, and (*b*) the whorl which is fixed on the spindle with the actual wheel. To attach this driving band, hold one end with the left hand, take the other end under and round the wheel, over and round groove E (Fig. 43). Now take it under and round the wheel again, then over and round the bobbin. Pull the ends

Fig. 41.—Spinning.

46

FIG. 42.—The spinning wheel.

tightly, and sew them firmly for about 1 inch with a needle and thread. Now, if the wool is held with the fingers at the point (F), and the wheel rotated by means of the pedal movement, two actions take place, viz. (1) the wool is twisted through the rotation of the spindle, and (2) it is wound on to the bobbin, because this is free on the spindle and revolves more rapidly owing to its groove having a smaller circumference than that on the spindle whorl. Having understood the principle on which the spinning wheel works, it is now necessary to practise the movements for spinning. A few minutes' practice in steady regular pedalling will be advisable, and the worker should learn to control the *stopping* of the movement. The wheel should be stopped when the pedal is just past its highest point, so that when the action is resumed the wheel does not reverse its movement, but starts off in the right direction without the need for pushing off with the hand.

Now the real spinning may be started. Take a length of *hand-spun* wool. Tie it on to the bobbin, carry it along the hooks of the 'fliers' (G) not previously mentioned, through the hole in the spindle, and out towards the worker. Twist on to this some wool from a 'rolag'. Now hold the wool near the spindle lightly with the left hand—the thumb on top and the first two fingers below, and work the pedal. With the right hand draw out a few inches of fleece,

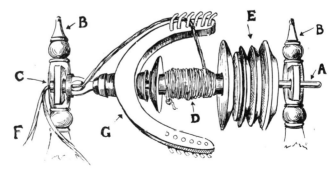

FIG. 43.—The spinning wheel spindle.

47

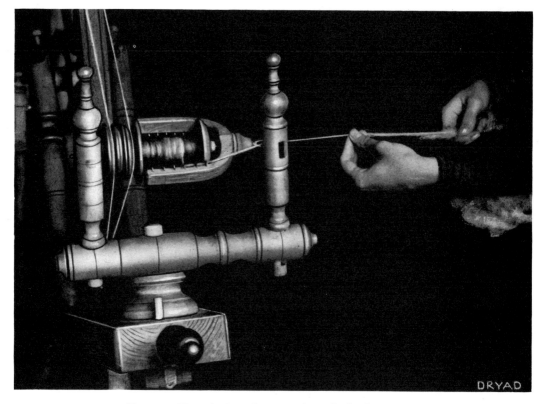

FIG. 44.—The spinning wheel, showing spinning in progress.

relax the hold of the left hand, and let the yarn run on to the bobbin. With practice it becomes possible to expose a longer and longer stretch of drawn-out fleece, and a delightfully rhythmical movement results as the right hand moves first from, and then towards, the left. But the beginner should not be too ambitious. Practice only will give the necessary skill. At first the yarn may be too fine or too coarse, or merely irregular; it may be overspun through being held too firmly and too long with the left hand, or insufficiently twisted and consequently weak. Sometimes the control of the twist will be relaxed and run up into the 'rolag', with disastrous results, and sometimes the thread will break. The beginner should work steadily with the aim of producing a thread not too fine, but regular in its thickness and twist. It is possible to obtain 2-ply as well as single-ply hand-spun wool—the former being much stronger though not necessarily harsher than the single-ply wool.

Two bobbins of single-ply wool of, as far as possible, an even tension, should first be spun. The two bobbins should then be placed on a spool rack, or if this is not available, the wool should be wound into two balls, each being placed in a box or jar on the floor. A length of wool should first be tied on to the bobbin, carried along the fliers G, threaded through the hole in the spindle and brought out towards the spinner at C.

The two ends of hand-spun wool should be twisted on to this as in the earlier spinning. The left hand should be held near to the opening C on the spindle to act as a guide only, the right hand being entirely responsible for the tension.

One thread should pass *over* the first finger and the second thread *between* the first and second finger of the left hand, to keep the threads apart. The two threads should then be held firmly together, between the thumb and first finger of the right hand. Extra tension can be acquired if necessary by passing the two threads over the first finger and under the second.

The pedal should now be worked but the wheel should revolve anti-clockwise—in the opposite direction from ordinary spinning—to avoid re-spinning wool which has been already spun.

The nearer the left hand is to the hole C, the closer the twist, whereas the further the left hand is held from C, the looser the twist. The length of the twist and tension can, with experience, be regulated to suit requirements. If the wool is held too long in the right hand it becomes over-twisted and vice-versa.

On completion of the plying of the yarn, the wool should be wound into hanks as before.

The hand-spun wool must now be wound into skeins, and is ready for washing and dyeing. To prevent the wool from tangling during these operations, the beginning and end of each skein must be carried loosely round the skein and tied on itself. In addition, four other pieces of wool should be tied *loosely* round the skein at intervals between these first two ties. The wool is washed by immersing it in a lather made from warm soft water and any good plain soap. The skeins should be moved up and down in the lather and drawn lightly through the hands but never rubbed or twisted. They are then rinsed several times in clear water, lightly squeezed (not wrung or twisted), shaken out, and hung out to dry.

For dyeing, vegetable dyes will of course be used. These were the only dyes known to the early weavers, and since we are following the development of the craft along historical lines, it is consistent to use primitive materials for dyestuffs. In addition, the colours produced by these means are softer and mellower, and harmonise with each other more readily than do those produced by the commercial dyestuffs. It is a fascinating thing to experiment in dyeing wool with these vegetable substances, and the beginner need not fear to attempt it, since it is very difficult to spoil the wool! True, the resulting colour is not always what was intended, but if not suitable for the immediate purpose it may be set aside for future use; and if the colour is patchy the woven article may be all the more pleasing. This is perhaps the only instance in all crafts-manship where a standard of imperfection can be tolerated, and such a standard is hard to justify except by results. Some most pleasing fabrics have been woven from wool which, regarded from the standpoint of good dyeing, fell very far short of perfection.

It is not within the scope of the present volume to deal comprehensively with the subject of dyeing and to give an exhaustive list of recipes. It must suffice to describe the use of some of the homely and most easily used materials, and to refer the reader to some good books on the subject for further information. It is a good plan when experimenting with dyes to make, for future reference, a careful report of what is done, i.e. the amount of wool, the amount of mordant, quantity of water, and length of time it is boiled in the first process, and in the second process the quantity of water, amount of dyestuff, and length of boiling. To these notes should be attached a specimen of the colour produced. This will serve as a useful guide when wanting the same colour again, or in the attempt to produce a slightly different shade.

In order that the wool may 'take' the dye, it must usually be subjected to a process known as 'mordanting', though a few dyes are 'substantive', i.e. need no mordant. The mordanting usually precedes the dyeing, but sometimes is done at the same time and sometimes afterwards. Alum is the most commonly used mordant, sometimes combined with cream of tartar; others are sulphate of iron (copperas), bichromate of potash, and tin crystals (stannous chloride). For both mordanting and dyeing it is essential to use the wool while still damp from the washing, or after it has been soaked in warm water.

To mordant with alum. For 1 lb. of wool dissolve 2 to 4 oz. of alum (according to the nature of the wool—less for fine soft wool, more for the coarser variety) in a large pot of cold water. Put the pot over the fire until the water is warm, then 'enter' the wool, and heat gradually to boiling point. Next, simmer gently for 45 to 60 minutes (again according to the nature of the wool, less time being necessary for fine wool). Leave the bath to cool overnight. Then lift the wool out with a stick and let it drain—squeeze gently, but do not wring or wash it, and put it away in a cool place for two or three days.

Brighter colours result if 1 oz. of cream of tartar is added to the alum.

The wool is now ready for dyeing. The results are better if it is kept for a day or two, but it should not be allowed to dry. The first experiments in dyeing should be with materials easily collected at home:

(1) Onion skins give a bright yellow if mordanted with alum. Save a small basketful of onion skins (about 1 lb. of skins for 1 lb. of wool) from the kitchen. Boil in water for an hour and allow to cool, then enter the mordanted wool, and boil for another hour. Rinse well and hang out to dry. Curiously enough there is no unpleasant smell! If stannous chloride is used as a mordant the resulting

colour is orange. For this purpose use $\frac{1}{4}$ oz. of mordant to 1 lb. of wool and allow the water in which it has been dissolved to get quite cold before entering the wool.

(2) Elderberries give a dull violet colour. Collect a large basketful of ripe berries and use in the same way as the onion skins.

(3) Walnut hulls give a variety of useful shades of fawn and brown. Collect the outer green shells when the nuts fall in autumn. Put them in water as they are collected. The longer they are kept the better the results. Use as above.

A few other dyestuffs can be collected in sufficient quantities to be useful for dyeing, and the reader may now like to experiment with a few of the following:

Leaves of privet, tomato, nettles, cow parsley, pear, weld (wild mignonette), cabbage, which produce varying shades of yellow and pale green, and walnut leaves which produce brown.

Fruits such as ivy berries, sloe, whortleberries, privet, elder, damsons, bryony, which give various shades of blue and purple.

Roots of sorrel, yellow ladies' bedstraw (giving red), bracken, nettle and dock (yellow), yellow iris (grey), dandelion (magenta). Dock roots also give grey and black with copperas as a mordant.

Bark of alder and elder, which produce black when mordanted with copperas, and of oak, producing green.

Young tips of heather and of bracken, both producing yellow.

Roots and bark should be cleaned, chopped up, and soaked for at least twenty-four hours before being used.

Leaves, etc., are put into cold water and boiled to extract the colour. A small quantity of alum is a help in this process. Then the wool is dyed in the strained infusion after this has been diluted if necessary. Large quantities of these dyestuffs are necessary, sometimes 1 lb. to 1 lb. of wool, but often 2 lb. or more of dyestuff to the pound.

Many other dyestuffs must be bought from a drysalter: i.e.

Fustic chips, which give bright yellow and old gold.

Logwood chips, which give greys, blues, purples, in combination with other dyes such as madder and with different mordants.

Cochineal, which gives pinkish-purple shades when mordanted with alum and scarlet if mordanted with tin crystals.

Cutch, which gives the reddish brown associated with the sails of fishing boats at sunset. This should be mordanted with $\frac{1}{4}$ oz. bichromate of potash dissolved in hot water and used as a rinse *after* the dyeing.

Madder gives delightful shades of red if used with mordants of alum and cream of tartar, and varieties of orange if mixed with fustic chips or flavin. Unfortunately, this is a rather expensive dyestuff, but is unequalled for the beauty of the colours produced.

E

Indigo gives blue. This is a substantive dye, but the colour is more lasting if an alum mordant is used. The indigo vat is difficult and perhaps dangerous for amateurs to prepare, since it necessitates the use of sulphuric acid. It is best to buy the dye ready prepared in the form of indigo paste, a dessertspoonful of which produces a good shade of blue, when used with enough water to cover 1 lb. of wool. The indigo vat gives better and more permanent colour and the more ambitious worker will find instructions for the preparation of this in any of the books on dyeing mentioned in the Bibliography.

For dyeing green the wool should be dyed blue with indigo, then yellow with fustic, flavin, or with onion skins. A great variety of shades can be produced by varying the strengths of the respective colours.

A few typical recipes are here given—in each case for 1 lb. wool.

GOLDEN YELLOW. *Mordant.* $\frac{1}{2}$ oz. bichromate of potash.

Dye. 2-6 oz. fustic, according to strength of colour desired.

The dye should be soaked overnight in water. Some workers enclose it in a muslin bag, but this is not essential.

Dissolve the mordant by heating in a little soft water in the dye bath. Add enough cold water to cover the wool. When lukewarm enter the wool, bring slowly to the boil and simmer for 30 minutes. Keep the bath covered during the whole of the above process. Add the dye-stuff and the water in which it was soaked. Boil gently for 30 minutes. Leave the bath to cool before removing the wool which must then be well rinsed and hung out to dry.

A paler *Lemon* yellow is produced by substituting 4 oz. alum for the bichromate of potash in the above recipe and using less fustic.

For an orange yellow use bichromate as before but add 1 oz. or more of madder to the dye-stuff.

MADDER RED. *Mordant.* 2-4 oz. alum. 1 oz. cream of tartar.

Dye. 8 oz. madder.

Mordant the wool for 30 to 45 minutes. It should then be hung in a bag for a few days, but kept damp.

Soak the madder overnight. Put it into the dye bath with enough water to cover the wool. When warm enter the wool and bring very slowly to the boil. Boil gently for 30 minutes, or until the desired colour is obtained. Rinse well. If a pink shade is required, the madder should be put in very hot water to kill the brown colouring matter.

CRIMSON. *Mordant.* 2 oz. alum. 1 oz. cream of tartar.

Dye. 1 oz. ground cochineal.

Mordant the wool for 30 minutes. Add the dye-stuff to the same bath and boil for a further 30 minutes. Rinse well.

SCARLET. *Mordant.* 1 oz. tin crystals. 1 oz. oxalic crystals.

Dye. 2 oz. cochineal.

52

Dissolve mordant and dyestuff together in the dye bath; add enough water to cover the wool. Enter the wool. Boil for 45 minutes. Rinse well. Care must be taken not to use too much stannous chloride, as this may spoil the texture of the wool.

DARK PURPLE. *Mordant.* 3 oz. alum. ½ oz. tartar.

Dye. 4 oz. logwood.

Mordant as before and keep it in a bag for two days. Soak the dye-stuff overnight in water. Put logwood and the water in which it was soaked into the dye bath, add enough water to cover the wool. When warm enter the wool. Boil for 30 minutes to 1 hour according to depth of colour required. Rinse well.

REDDISH BROWN. *Mordant.* ½ oz. bichromate of potash.

Dye. 2 oz. cutch.

Dissolve the dye-stuff in water, add enough water to cover the wool. When warm enter the wool, which must be damp. Boil for 1 hour. Rinse in hot water in which the mordant has been dissolved.

This brief account of vegetable dyes cannot be concluded without mentioning the lichens. These require no mordant. They are gathered from rocks, stones, and trees, and under the name of 'Crottal' or 'Crottle' are still largely used in country districts by weavers interested in vegetable dyeing, and are responsible for the comfortable smell of home-spun tweeds. To dye with lichens allow 1 lb. to 1 lb. of wool. Put the lichen in a large pot and fill with cold water. Bring this to the boil and simmer for 3 hours, and leave to cool overnight. Next day, having soaked the wool thoroughly, put it into the pot, and boil all together until the desired colour is obtained. Leave until cold, then wash the wool and shake out the lichen. The following are some commonly used lichens:

Parmelia saxatilis (Crottle): dyes orange-brown. Found on rocks near the sea in Scotland and Shetland.

Parmelia omphalodes (Black Crottle): dyes red-brown. Found on rocks. Dartmoor, Welsh mountains, and Scottish highlands.

Parmelia parietina: bright yellow lichen found on stone walls and the roofs of old buildings. Dyes yellow-brown.

Lecanora tartarea: dyes red. Grows on limestone rocks.

Sticta pulmonacea (Oak Rag or Lung-wort): dyes orange. Found on trees in England and Scotland.

Ramalina scapuloram: dyes yellow and yellow-brown. A common grey lichen. Grows on old stone walls near the sea and on trees in damp woods.

It is hoped that the reader has by this time become interested in the possibilities of vegetable dyeing, and will turn to the fuller accounts to be found in books dealing exclusively with the subject; also that she will experience for herself the pleasure of experiment and discovery.

CHAPTER VI

Labour-Saving

"The whole earth is full of monuments to nameless inventors."—MASON.

HITHERTO all the work suggested has been done with coarse materials, and now the weaver is ambitious to work with wool. Very small pieces of work may still be done on cardboard foundations, but for finer fibres the warp threads must be much closer together. If threaded through the cardboard in the same way as the raffia warps, they tend to tear the cardboard. In order to avoid this the holes should be made alternately on the upper and lower of two lines placed both at the top and bottom of the card (Fig. 45); or if very fine warping is required, they may even be arranged as in the photographs, Fig. 15, illustrating experiments with pattern. This latter method is still used in some factories for experimental work. It is obvious from the picture that a finished edge at top and bottom will not be possible and the superfluous ends of warp must be dispensed with before making up the article. Small articles, such as pin cushions, covers for needle books, pen wipers, and kettle holders may be woven in this way, and afford a further opportunity for the use of small 'all-over' patterns, such as were described in Chapter III. Incidentally, they bring the weaver on to a further stage in the development of the craft, i.e. the desire for time- and labour-saving.

The worker, whether adult or child, is now in a position to understand the attitude of the primitive weaver who, having mastered the routine work of simple weaving, invented methods of decoration, and learnt to produce spun fibres, became wearied with the monotony of always going under and over the individual threads of a wide warp. If only there might be some way of picking up all the required threads at once and so carrying the weft under the whole number of them in one operation!

Prior to this the early weaver had probably already made use of a device, which has since become common in all weaving looms, viz. the use of two flat sticks threaded into the warp just as two rows of weaving would be done, one stick going under an alternate set of strands, say the odd numbers, and the other under the even numbers. These were found necessary in order to keep the strands separate when a wide warp was used. Now, if one of these sticks (the one nearest to the spot where the weft is inserted) was turned on edge, it raised a whole set of alternate warp strands, thus producing an opening or 'shed' through which the weft could be passed. This 'shed stick' then is the first labour-saving device, and at any rate alternate rows of weaving could be

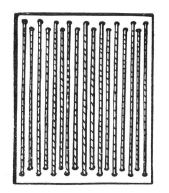

FIG. 45.—Arrangement of warp
on cardboard for finer work.

FIG. 46.—Simple shuttle.

done in one operation, leaving the intermediate rows to be done by the old method of weaving under one and over one. It is a common thing for pupils who have arrived at this idea to suggest using the second stick in the same way. A moment's experiment will suffice to show that this will not work, because the stick nearer the weaving goes over a set of strands and prevents them from being lifted by the farther stick.

For a long time no doubt the early weaver was content with labour-saving in alternate rows of weaving, but meanwhile the possibility of further improvements in that direction was being considered. Our pupils should work along similar lines.

The pupils have also, by this time, almost certainly discovered, as had their early predecessors, the need for another appliance—the shuttle. The continuous length of weft has been discovered to be unmanageable, and they have wrapped it round a long thin piece of cardboard or wood. Some such form of shuttle was used by many early weavers, and is still in use by primitive people today. Probably the most convenient form is that illustrated in Fig. 46.

Now, the weaver, still working unconsciously along much the same lines as her early predecessors, will probably discover that instead of picking up the alternate threads (those which go under the shed stick) one at a time she can save time by hooking up several threads with the little finger of the left hand and threading the shuttle under the whole group thus raised. This leads to the invention of *leashes* and *leash rods*, which combine to form the earliest kind of *heddle*. The leashes are loops of fibre tied to each of the alternate strands which are not picked up by the shed stick. These loops are slipped on to a rod, which, when raised, picks up the whole of these strands, thus forming the desired *second shed*. After the shuttle has been taken across, the rod is placed down on the warp, thus allowing these strands to resume their original position, when the other set may be raised by means of the shed stick. Labour-saving by this method was most probably practised by the Egyptians some 5,000 years ago, and by using it on the simple piece of apparatus here described, and which has been previously used without labour-saving devices (see Chapter II), the modern weaver will be able to produce useful pieces of material much more quickly than has hitherto been possible. This 'board loom', or a simple frame which serves the same purpose, may be bought, or can easily be made as follows:

55

Take a flat piece of wood of any available size up to about 10 inches by 16 inches and ½ inch thick. On to each end of this nail a piece of wood 1½ inches wide and 1 inch longer than the width of the board, in such a position that it projects ½ inch beyond the width of the board at each side, and ¼ inch beyond the upper and lower surfaces (Fig. 47a). Sandpaper all surfaces to prevent the wool from catching. For the warp use 3- or 4-ply wool. To make a warp which can easily be drawn round the board so that the whole of it can be used, proceed as follows: Lay a stick or piece of ½-inch dowel rod across the board. Tie an end of the warp to this, carry the warp to one end of the board A under it, and down the board to B, then up to the stick, round this, and back to B along the board to A down to stick, round it, and back to A, and so on until enough threads have been warped, when the end is again tied to the stick (see Fig. 47b).

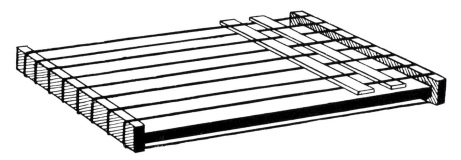

FIG. 47a.—Home-made flat board loom.

This is the under surface of the board loom. The spacing gauge mentioned in Chapter II may be used, or small nails may be driven into the projecting ledge at the end B of the loom at distances of ½ inch apart to regulate the warp threads. If 3-ply wool is used, there should be 14 of these to the inch, but for 4-ply wool, jute, or thick cotton 10 or 12 to the inch will suffice. Before starting to weave push the stick up to the end A of the loom, turn this over, and start work at this end. Now take two narrow flat sticks, rather longer than the width of the work. Having drilled a small hole in each end of these, thread the first under one set of alternate threads and the second under the others. Tie a string through the hole, and from end to end of each stick to

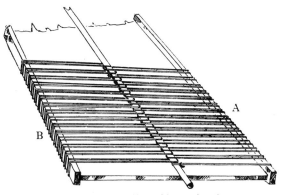

FIG. 47b.—Underside of board loom showing more practical method of fixing warp.

keep them from slipping out. Now, if the lower of these sticks is turned on edge it raises a set of strands, making a shed through which the shuttle may be passed. To produce the second shed we must attach a loop of thin string or soft cotton to each of the threads which the stick does not raise. To ensure these being all of the same length, place on the warp a 12-inch rule, or flat piece of wood or cardboard, and take each loop under the warp thread and round the cardboard, and tie the ends. This is now removed, and the loops slipped on to a thick stick, which, if raised, will lift all the threads and produce the required shed. Another method, which may be found simpler, is to cut a number of strings 11 inches long, tie the two ends of each string together with a reef knot, taking care always to use up the same length in the tying, slip a double end under a warp thread and then pass the other double end through the loop made by the first one (Fig. 48a). A stick is then threaded through all the long loops.

It may be found quicker and more satisfactory, instead of tying each leash separately, to make them continuous in the following way:

FIG. 48a.—Method of making leashes.

To one end of the stick which is being used as a gauge, tie a piece of string, carry this along the edge nearest to the weaver, and tie at the other end of the stick. Now take the leash thread, tie it to this string at the extreme left, carry it over and then under the gauge, round the first warp thread which it is necessary to raise to form the second shed, and make one, two, or more blanket stitches on the string (according to the distance apart of the warp strands) (Fig. 48b). Repeat this process until all the necessary strands have been looped. The gauge is now removed, leaving the leashes all connected up on the string, and into these a thinner stick is inserted as a leash rod.

FIG. 48b.—Method of making continuous leashes.

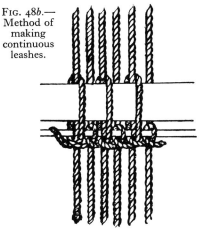

The actual weaving is now perfectly simple to anyone who has done the previous work. To make the second shed more effective, the ruler can be quickly inserted when the leash rod is raised, so as to leave the weaver's hands free to use the shuttle. This ruler also serves to beat up the work. Care must be taken not to pull the weft too tightly and so make the work too narrow. As the weaving proceeds the work is pulled round the frame, and the length of material produced may be just a little less than double the length of the frame. Stripes may be inserted in

FIG. 49a.—SUGGESTIONS FOR THE USE OF MATERIALS WOVEN ON SMALL LOOMS.

FIG. 49b.—SUGGESTIONS FOR THE USE OF MATERIALS WOVEN ON SMALL LOOMS.

warp and weft, and plaid patterns produced. If other decorations are desired the worker must leave the heddles for a time and work with the needle in the way described in Chapter III.

By this means she is now able to make fairly quickly such articles as small scarves, hatbands, ties, pochettes, dress trimmings; or the woven strips may be joined by means of decorative stitching and made into larger work bags, etc. (See illustrations of such work in Figs. 49a and 49b, and the board loom in use in Fig. 53).

This simple arrangement of shed sticks and leashes is characteristic of very many of the primitive looms of the past, and is still used very largely today. The actual looms vary somewhat in structure, and may be horizontal or vertical but in the great majority labour-saving is effected, first, by means of the shed stick, and secondly, by means of the leashes. This is clearly shown in Figs. 50, 51 and 52 (reproduced, with permission, from *Primitive Looms :* Ling Roth).

Many of the beautiful Persian rugs are woven by means of equipment no more elaborate than this.

Some weavers use two sets of leashes, one picking up each alternate set of threads, but it is obvious that the use of a shed stick, as described above, is

59

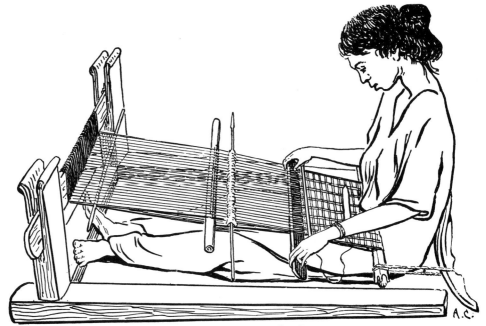

Fig. 50.—Bali woman at her loom.

simpler, and makes the second set of leashes unnecessary. At a later stage, however, when the worker is ready to weave patterns, as many as four sets of leashes may be used in just the same way as is described for the four-heddle loom in Chapter IX. Such pattern work cannot be dealt with in this chapter, but the reader is reminded that all the instructions for pattern work in Chapter IX apply equally to the loom here described if it is fitted with four sets of leashes.

Fig. 51.—Santa Cruz weaver.

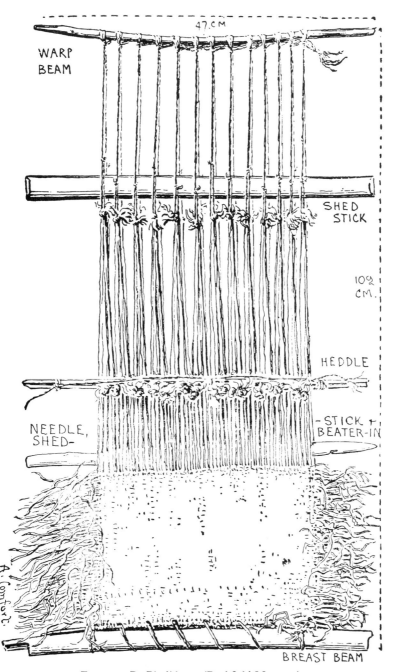

FIG. 52.—Ba-Pindi loom (Bankfield Museum).

61

FIG. 53.—BOARD LOOM IN USE WITH LEASHES.

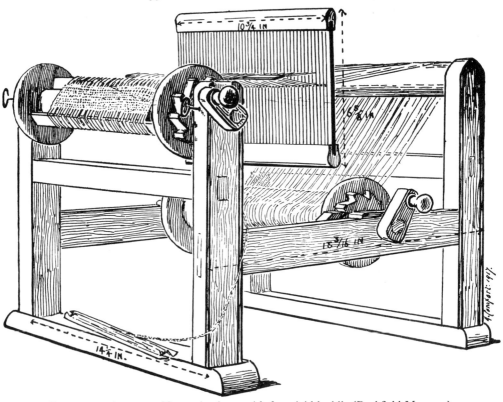

FIG. 54.—20th century Norwegian loom with free rigid heddle (Bankfield Museum).

And now we come to another fascinating labour-saving device —the use of the rigid heddle. There is no definite information as to the period of history at which this evolved, but it has been used by primitive peoples such as the Lapps, and the Pueblo Indians, and is still used in the making of braids, belts, etc., in Germany and America. This heddle (Fig. 55a) is made of bone, wood, or metal. Sometimes it is cut from a thin sheet of material and sometimes made up of separate slats fastened on to a frame. The threading of this is simplicity itself—one warp thread goes through a hole in the rigid strip, the next in between two strips, and so on. When the whole heddle is raised the threads passing through the strips are raised, while the others which are free in the spaces remain in position, thus forming the first shed (Fig. 55b). When the heddle is depressed the attached threads go below the free ones, and form a second shed (Fig. 55c).

It is obvious that for this purpose the shallow loom which has hitherto been used will not suffice, since it would be impossible to depress the heddle. We shall therefore make use of an old box. Any light wooden box will serve, provided that it is deep enough to admit of the heddle being pushed down sufficiently far to form a shed.

FIG. 55a.—Rigid heddle made from strips of wood.

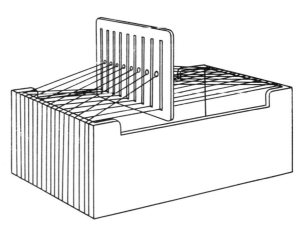

FIG. 55b.—Rigid heddle raised.

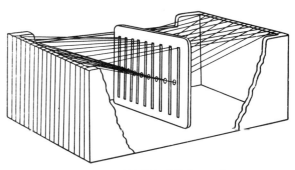

FIG. 55c.—Rigid heddle lowered.

63

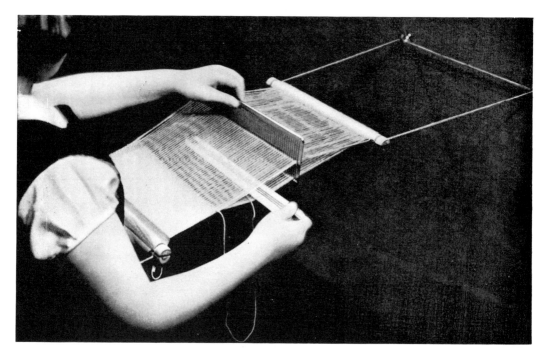

FIG. 56a.—WEAVING WITH SMALL METLYX RIGID HEDDLE.

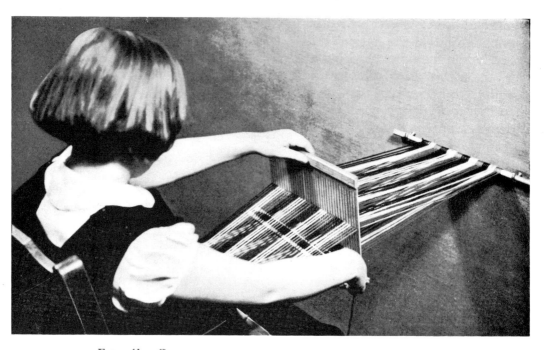

FIG. 56b.—CHILD WORKING WITH LARGE WOODEN RIGID HEDDLE.

64

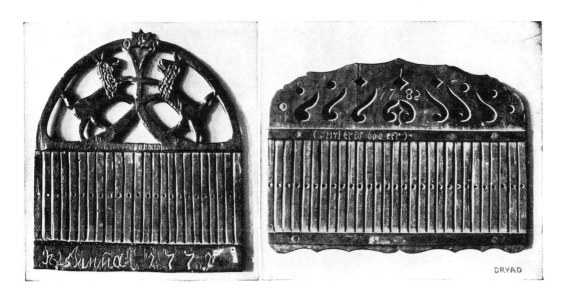

FIG. 57.—NORWEGIAN LOOMS.

This rigid heddle has the advantage of serving also as a 'beater-in' for the weft, and it also helps in regulating the width of the work. A twentieth-century Norwegian loom making use of this device is illustrated in Fig. 54.

Having discovered some possibilities of the rigid heddle, it is pleasing to find that this alone may now serve as a loom without any frame at all! The photographs in Fig. 57 show two beautiful eighteenth-century Norwegian looms which were no doubt used in this way, while Figs. 56a and 56b show children making use of the same device. It is a method frequently found amongst primitive peoples, and is used in Germany today for weaving narrow braids and belts. To set up this 'Waist Loom' with the rigid heddle proceed as follows: cut the required number of threads of even length by winding round two posts clamped to a table (Fig. 58) or round two large nails driven into a bench. Remember to allow for waste in tying on at each end, and for the last few inches of warp on which it is difficult to weave. Ten inches at least should be added to the required length of the finished article. Prop up the heddle in a clamp (Fig. 59) or between books. Place the warp behind the heddle (away from the worker) and bring the threads to the front, alternately through a hole and a slot. As each thread comes through it is tied to a strong flat stick or dowel rod. The best method of doing this is by a 'clove hitch' knot (details of which are given in Fig. 60). This has the advantage that it can be slipped off the stick without

65

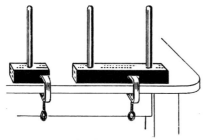

FIG. 58.—Warping posts.

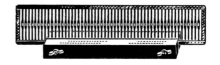

FIG. 59.—Clamp for supporting rigid
heddle during threading.

untying when the work is finished, leaving ends to form a fringe. A quicker method of procedure up to this point but lacking this advantage claimed for the 'clove-hitch' knot is as follows:—assuming the warp to have been wound on posts or nails—cut the threads at one end. Now take the double end of each thread and wrap round a stick, threading the cut ends through the loop. Proceed until the whole warp is mounted. Then thread through the heddle. When the whole warp is threaded, the stick is placed in position behind two nails driven into the bench or tied to two hooks in a wall. The weaver now takes another stick, ties a string to one end of it, carries the string around her waist, and ties it to the other end of the stick. The warp threads are now taken in order, in bunches of about four at a time, and tied to this stick in the manner indicated in Chapter VIII, Fig. 97. The weaver must sit at the requisite distance from the point where the first stick is fixed, and take care to see that the same warp tension is kept throughout. It is best to tie one bunch on the

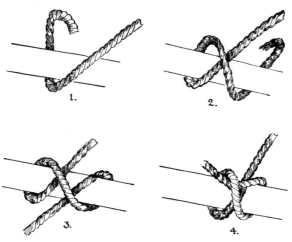

1.

2.

3.

4.

FIG. 60.—Clove-hitch knot.

left-hand side, then one on the right, and so on. (For a very long warp with many threads, it would be well to use the method of Chapter VIII to the point indicated in Fig. 95, then roll up the warp temporarily on these sticks, thread the heddle, unroll the warp, fix the back stick, and tie on as indicated above.) The waist loom is now ready for work. By moving the body the weaver produces the necessary warp tension. Before starting the weaving a flat stick is woven

66

into the warp, against which the weft may be beaten up by means of the rigid heddle. As the work grows it may be rolled up on the rod and stick and held in place by another stick laid under the roll and tied at each end to the first stick. The heddle in Fig. 55a is made of plywood, and will weave a fabric up to 9 inches wide. It is necessarily coarse, having 8 threads to the inch (4 going through holes and 4 between the strips). It is suitable for using with thick 4-ply wool, which admits of quickly growing work, and will produce material suitable for children's or men's scarves, small table runners, and for making up into hot-water bottle covers, bags, pochettes, and such articles. If threaded with warp of alternate colours and woven with a third colour, a delightful effect is produced. The pouffe shown in Fig. 61 was made from strips of material woven in this way with the heddle described, and Fig. 62 shows several useful articles made in a similar way. Such a heddle may easily be made. Procure some $\frac{1}{8}$-inch strip wood $\frac{3}{16}$-inch wide, and some $\frac{5}{8}$-inch wide. Of the latter, cut four strips each 9 inches long, and of these place two in a horizontal position parallel to each other at a distance of $5\frac{1}{2}$ inches apart. Fix them temporarily by nailing through to a board. Cut the narrow strips into lengths of $6\frac{3}{4}$ inches (36 required), now glue one of these into position at one end of the two parallel strips, and, using a fine nail as a 'spacer', glue on all the other strips at equal distances apart. Now take the two wider strips and glue over the first two, thus encasing the ends of the narrow ones. Place a board or book on these to keep them in position until dry, and then drive in some tiny panel pins at each of the ends, and at intervals along top and bottom for additional security. Now mark the centre point of the strips by a line going right across, place cardboard or wood underneath to support them and drill or burn the hole in each strip.

Other heddles (known as Metlyx heddles), in a variety of sizes and made of metal, may be purchased. They take 13 threads to the inch, and are suitable for use with 2- and 3-ply wool, knitting cotton and similar yarns. The smaller ones will make braids, belts, ties, and trimmings, while the larger ones will make scarves, etc. It is not wise to attempt to use a greater width than 9 inches with the waist-loom method, but the ones 15 inches and 20 inches wide may be used on one or other of the frame looms (Figs. 63, 84a, 87 and 88). This method of weaving is to be recommended for school use, as the apparatus is simple, costs little, occupies little space, and can easily be carried about. Children can very easily and quickly weave their own school hatbands, tunic girdles, or the coloured strips worn by games teams.

Another method of weaving without a loom is by using a shed stick and leashes instead of a rigid heddle. A long warp is made by a series of single threads, the ends of each being tied together after the thread has been carried right round two rods.

F

FIG. 61.—POUFFE MADE FROM STRIPS OF COARSE MATERIAL WOVEN WITH RIGID-HEDDLE WAIST LOOM.

One of these is tied to the wall, the other attached by a string to the weaver's waist. This method enables a great number of warp threads to be used for each inch of work, and so make it possible to introduce *warp* patterns, such as were described in Chapter III. The braids photographed in Fig. 16 are examples of the work which may be produced by this method. They may be worn as ties, and were once used for wrapping round the trousers at the top of the boots, by skiers

FIG. 62.—ARTICLES WOVEN WITH RIGID-HEDDLE WAIST LOOM.

68

in the winter sports districts in Germany. The examples photographed are 1 inch wide, and have 32 warp threads.

And now, since the rigid heddle is not easily produced on such a fine scale as to enable fine work to be done, i.e., work requiring a warp with more than 14 threads to the inch, it becomes necessary to consider a method of achieving such work by more expeditious means. On the simple board loom described at the beginning of this chapter, leashes were tied on to each alternate warp thread; this is a tiresome process, which must be repeated with each new warp. (If the method of continuous leashes is used, it is just possible, though difficult and tiresome, to use these for another warp, threading each alternate strand through a leash whilst carrying the warp round the board.)

An effort must now therefore be made to provide some more permanent equipment in the form of heddles and heddle strings, which can be used again and again. Two such heddles will be made, each of which will raise an alternate set of warp strands. The weaver will realise that one would suffice—one set of strands being raised by means of the shed stick—but it will be advisable at this stage to practise the use of two heddles in preparation for the four-heddle loom to be used later for pattern weaving.

For the loom a box will be used, with a portion of the sides removed so as not to interfere with the passing of the shuttle (see illustration of box with rigid heddle, Fig. 55b), but the box need not be so deep for this purpose, as each heddle will only be raised, not lowered; or a framework, such as is illustrated in Fig. 63, may easily be constructed from light stripwood. The heddles

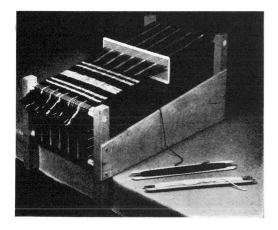

FIG. 63.—Simple loom without rollers for use with leashes, home-made string heddles or bought rigid heddle.

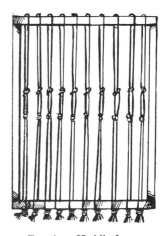

FIG. 64.—Heddle frame.

consist of strings[1] of uniform length, with a loop in the centre through which certain warp strands will pass, and they will be fixed on to a framework made from thin strips of plywood (Fig. 64). The heddle strings must be long enough to give sufficient 'play' to the free warp strands so as to form an adequate shed, but their centre loop must not be higher than the top of the box or frame, so that if the box used is 2½ inches deep, the heddles must be 5 inches long. To make them, drive two 1½-inch nails, without heads, into a piece of wood at a distance of 5 inches apart. Mark the centre point between these nails, and in the same straight line, drive in two others, each about ⅜-inch from the centre (see Fig. 65).

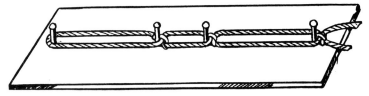

FIG. 65.—Method of making string healds.

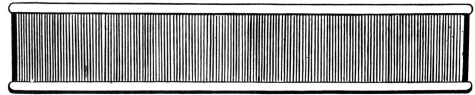

FIG. 66.—Reed.

With this simple equipment any number of heddle strings can be made. Take some very fine string or cotton, a little longer than twice the length of the required heddle, fold it in half and take the bend round the top nail. Take the two ends, one on either side of the second nail, beneath it, and tie tightly with a reef or any non-slip knot. Now take them below the third nail, tie again, then below the fourth, and tie. Repeat for as many strings as are required. This number depends on the width of the fabric and the number of warp threads to the inch. For a piece of material 10 inches wide, with 16 threads to the inch, we should need 80 strings on each of two heddles. Thread through top and bottom loops of these 80 strings strips of thin wood, then, stretching these to their utmost extent, get someone to hold them whilst other strips of wood, the length of the strings, are nailed on to the ends at right angles, so making a rigid rectangular frame (Fig. 64). The two heddles are now complete, and in the process of carrying the warp round the frame two strands will be threaded through the loop on the first heddle, the next two *between* the first and second strings on this heddle and through the first loop on the second heddle. These

---

[1]Heddle strings or wires are also known as healds, headles and yelds.

threads have been used double to give strength to the selvedge. This process is repeated with single threads, until the whole warp has been threaded, except the last four, which must be used double for the second selvedge, and the loom is now ready for work. The weaver is now able to produce weaving of much finer texture, for which 2-ply wool, cotton, or linen thread may be used. The size of the work is of course determined by the loom, which may be of any width, and the length of the fabric may be a few inches shorter than the distance round the entire box or frame. For beating up the work a flat stick may be inserted into the shed after each pass of the weft and pressed close to the work, or a fine comb may be used; but the best work is produced if a proper *reed* is used. This reed was an appliance used quite early in the development of the weaver's craft, but hitherto has not been necessary, since the shed stick or rigid heddle has served the purpose. It had two uses—for keeping the warp equally spaced and for beating up the work. It owes its name to the fact that it was originally made from a series of reeds fastened together at top and bottom, the warp threads being carried *between* the reeds. This was only suitable for coarse work, and the modern reeds are made from strips of fine steel fastened into a framework (Fig. 66).

In general use for coarse work, one thread is passed through each dent of the reed (with an additional thread in the first two and last two dents of the reed) to give added strength at the selvedges.

For finer work (20 or more threads to the inch) it is advisable to use a reed with half the number of dents, e.g. for 28 threads to the inch—a 14 dent reed) —putting two threads through every dent.

This avoids undue friction and moreover economises on the number of reeds necessary in a weaver's equipment.

To illustrate the latter point an example is given of the various ways in which a reed can be used:

8 dent reed—One thread in alternate dents	..	4 threads to inch
One thread in every dent ..	..	8 ,, ,,
One and two threads alternately	..	12 ,, ,,
Two threads in each dent..	..	16 ,, ,,
Three threads in each dent	..	24 ,, ,,

Other examples can be worked out by a weaver for a 10, 12, 14 reed, etc.

This method of using a coarser reed and putting two or more threads in each dent of the reed in preference to a finer reed with one thread per dent, is largely used in the weaving mills without any detriment to the resulting fabric.

A loom embodying a different form of labour-saving device is the Scottish Inkle Loom (Fig. 67). At this loom the weaver sits comfortably on a chair, and can weave very rapidly. Braids and girdles may be made with 3- or 4-ply wool or knitting cotton; or rug wool is made into strips which are sewn together to

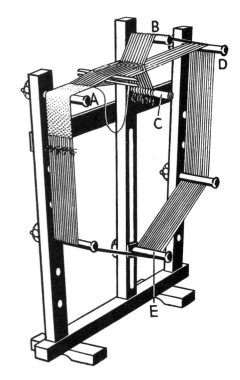

FIG. 67.—DRYAD INKLE LOOM.

FIG. 68.—MAT MADE FROM STRIPS WOVEN ON INKLE LOOM

make attractive mats (see Fig. 68). On this loom the warp is closely packed, the weft is not beaten very closely together, and only the warp is seen in the finished braid. It offers scope for interesting experiments with warp patterns (Figs. 15 and 16). In 6-ply rug wool forty warp threads were required to make the 3-inch strips sewn together to make the mat in Fig. 68, while in thick coloured knitting cotton or 4-ply wool, forty-eight threads will make a braid or girdle $1\frac{1}{2}$ inches wide. With brightly coloured cottons junior scholars can easily make for themselves the different-coloured braids worn by teams in the physical training class.

To fit up the loom, place one peg in the hole at the top of the frame (right-hand side), one in a lower hole on the same side, and another opposite to this on the left side. (In the diagram, the pegs are fixed in the third hole from the bottom but this position can be altered to suit the length of warp required.)

Then put peg A in the hole at the top of the left upright: the grooved peg B in the hole at the top of the centre upright and peg C (on which the heddle strings are fixed) in the hole immediately below this.

The first warp thread is taken from peg A through the first heddle string on peg C (away from the worker), over the grooved peg B, round peg D (top right), down and round the two lower pegs and back to A, where it is tied on itself.

The next thread goes straight from A, across and round peg D, down and round the two lower pegs and back to A, where it is tied as before. The third thread follows the same course as the first but passes through the second heddle string. The fourth follows the second and so on until sufficient threads have been warped.

Another peg E is now placed over the warp at the foot of the loom, inserted in the slot in the centre upright and adjusted to produce the necessary tension.

Now the shuttle is wound with weft of the same colour as the outer warp threads. The shed is formed by pressing down or raising the warp with the hand placed above or below it at the right-hand side of the heddle. When the weaving has proceeded so far that a shed can no longer be produced, the whole warp may be drawn round the loom to the desired position, after removing peg E.

It may be worth noting that the Inkle Loom may actually be made to serve the purpose of a warping board. To do this, merely remove the peg containing heddle strings and insert other pegs as required.

CHAPTER VII

Rug-Weaving

THE weaver may now like to try her hand at rug-weaving. A large, old picture frame, provided it is strong, or wood made up into this form, will serve as a loom, and will be large enough to make doormats, small rugs, and bedside strips. The warp will be of string or soft cotton yarn. This is taken round and round the picture frame, not too tightly, but with an even tension, and spaced at not more than 5 threads to the inch. In case the warp may be too loose for easy working at any stage, it may be well to place a thin strip of wood flat against the end of the frame before warping. Then, if necessary, other strips of wood may be driven in between this and the frame, so tightening the warp. (If only a small mat is desired the warp may be taken simply from top to bottom and back, being carried through small staples driven into the frame.)

Shed stick and leashes are arranged as described in the previous chapter. This represents the essential minimum of equipment for rug-weaving, but it will be well worth while to take a little more trouble and fix up a frame in the way illustrated in Fig. 69.

A bar (A) is fixed by tying it with strong string a few inches from the top beam of the frame. For this bar a piece of a broom handle or of $1\frac{1}{4}$-inch dowel rod may be used. In the illustration it consists of a strong cardboard roll, such as is used for packing. The warp is carried round and round the frame, but the strands on the front of the frame are taken alternately under and over this roller, thus making a permanent shed. To facilitate the making of the leashes another roller (B) is fixed on small brackets or angle irons screwed on to the front of the frame about 7 inches from the top. The leashes should be made of strong thin twine, and they repay the trouble of making, since they are permanent, and the warp for a further piece of work need only be threaded through them. To make the leashes, first tie a length of strong string from end to end of bar B (Fig. 69). Now take a thin rod of wood

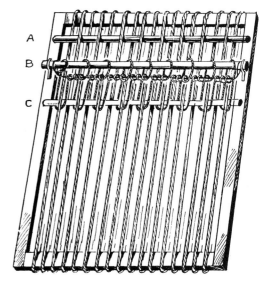

FIG. 69.—Home-made frame loom for rug-weaving showing method of making leashes.

FIG. 70.—DRYAD RUG LOOM.

FIG. 71.—Metal
beater for
beating down
weft.

or metal (C) rather longer than the width of the frame, and weave it into the warp, taking it *under* the strands which are under bar A. Fix it temporarily to the frame 8 inches below bar B. Now tie the leash cord to the end of the string on bar B, beginning at the left. Take it under the bar, down and under rod C and the first warp strand which it supports, back over the bar, and make three or more blanket stitches on the string, then under bar B down to bar C and under it and its next warp thread, up to bar B, and make three more blanket stitches on the string. Continue until all the necessary warp threads have been looped up. Rod C may now be removed. Rod B remains in position. The work is too wide to lift all alternate warp strands at once, and the shed is made by pulling a group of leashes forward with one hand while the shuttle is taken under with the other. Before starting the actual work weave in a flat stick, going under one set of alternate threads. This gives a firm edge against which the first weft may be beaten down. For beating down, a heavy comb will be needed, such as that illustrated in Fig. 71. As the work grows it is pulled round the frame, and the resulting mat can thus be almost as long as double the length of the frame.

The loom illustrated in Fig. 70 is a bought loom embodying the same ideas as the above, but is larger and stronger, is made to stand independently on the floor, and is equipped with an arrangement for altering the tension of the warp. With this equipment may be made flat woven rugs or pile rugs or, with finer materials, tapestries for cushion squares or for re-covering the seats of old chairs and stools. For the former the weft will be of rug wool, thrums (remnants from a carpet factory) or even torn-up rags. Beginners may also be interested to know that their first efforts at spinning may be used. Very beautiful rugs may be made from hand-spun wool which is very coarse and loosely spun. Some very cosy motor rugs have been made from strips woven on a loom and sewn together. In these cases the warp was of thick 4-ply or a thick singly-ply machine-spun wool about six to eight threads to the inch and the weft of coarse hand-spun wool, all vegetable dyed. Pleasing mats may also be made with rush or a variety of other materials on a string or cotton warp.

Rug-weaving is akin to tapestry-weaving. The characteristic of this is that the warp is entirely covered by the weft, hence the warp threads must be fairly far apart, the weft loosely inserted, and the rows of weaving tightly packed. To obtain the right tension, the weft thread, after passing through each group of warp strings, is left in an arched position, and then beaten down with the point of the shuttle to the preceding row.

At first any attempt at pattern must be confined to horizontal stripes produced by changing the weft. When other patterns are desired a new problem presents itself. We can no longer produce simple patterns by weaving under and over more than one warp thread or the warp would show. Some interesting patterns peculiar to this type of weave can, however, be produced by alternating, or otherwise varying, the order in which two or more colours are used, and experiments with this will give some attractive results. Such patterns are similar to the warp patterns described in Chapter III, but produced in the opposite way, i.e. in one case only the warp shows and makes the pattern : in the other the warp is entirely covered and the pattern is produced by the weft. The rug illustrated in Fig. 82 is a good example of this type of work. The same technique may also be applied to other materials and is useful where a tough fabric is desired. The evening bag material, Fig. 78 was made in this way.

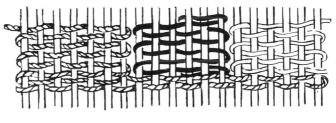

FIG. 72a.—Slits in weaving.

In order to understand the principle of pattern in tapestry-weaving the reader should draw up a warp of raffia or wool on cardboard, then try to weave so that a block of one colour, say blue, extends one-third of the way across. Green covers another third and yellow the other. Obviously each coloured weft must travel a certain distance across the warp and then return, and the result is a slit in the work wherever two colours meet (Fig. 72a). To avoid this we may link one colour into the other by either of the methods illustrated (Figs. 72b and 72c), but this makes the work very slow. If using a fine weft, we may overcome the difficulty by taking the two colours round the same warp thread, or, as some of the old tapestry workers did, we may weave a binder thread (a row of plain or tabby weave) of very fine material in between the rows of pattern. This was the method adopted in the ancient Peruvian tapestry illustrated in Fig. 76a. The slit is not a serious fault if it is only the

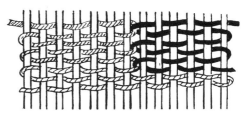

FIG. 72b.—Method of avoiding slits in weaving.

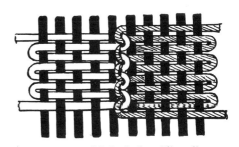

FIG. 72c.—Method of avoiding slits.

Fig. 73.—Dryad upright foot-power rug loom.

Fig. 74a.—Pile rug.

Fig. 74b.—Woven rug without pile.

length of three or four rows of weft, but otherwise it weakens the fabric. The reader should take an opportunity to examine any old piece of tapestry to find out whether the worker (1) has linked the colours when they meet, (2) has sewn up the slit afterwards, (3) has ignored it, or (4) has used a pattern not involving vertical lines. The latter is certainly the wisest plan for the amateur, who may now set to work to make a simple pattern for a rug which may include horizontal stripes, diagonal lines, and indented borders, such as are illustrated in Fig. 75.

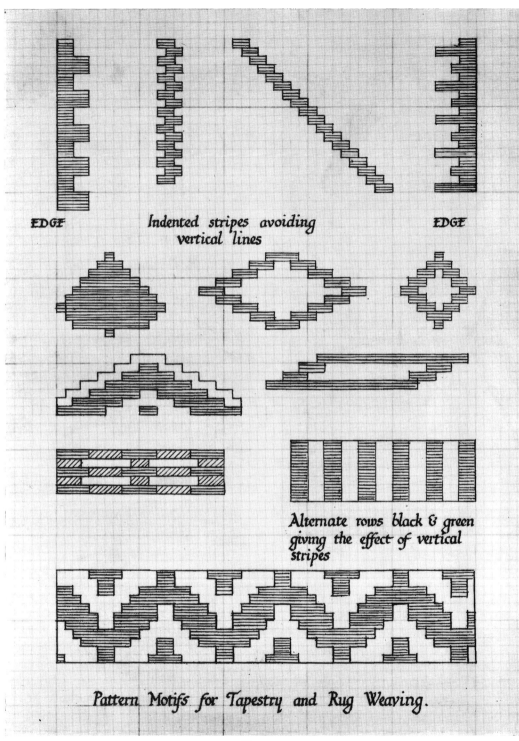

EDGE   *Indented stripes avoiding vertical lines*   EDGE

Alternate rows black & green giving the effect of vertical stripes

Pattern Motifs for Tapestry and Rug Weaving.

FIG. 75.

80

FIG. 76*a*.—FRAGMENT OF ANCIENT PERUVIAN TAPESTRY, *circa* 600 A.D.

FIG. 76*b*.—FRAGMENTS OF ANCIENT PERUVIAN TAPESTRY, *circa* 600 A.D.

81

FIGS. 77a AND b.—FRONT AND BACK OF MOORISH HANDBAG WORKED IN TAPESTRY.

FIG. 77c.—STOOL TOP IN TAPESTRY WEAVING ON HOME-MADE LOOM.

FIG. 78.—MATERIAL FOR EVENING BAG.

It is perhaps easier to design for *pile rugs*, since different colours in the pile can be added at any part without the difficulties experienced in changing the weft colour in a woven rug. This is an advantage, since it facilitates the breaking up of large masses of colour which are apt to give a hard effect in the woven rug unless colours are very carefully chosen; nevertheless, the weaver is advised to keep her patterns simple.

FIG. 79.—PEASANT WEAVING FROM FINE COTTON, SHOWING BORDERS OF TAPESTRY-
WEAVING, AND DECORATIONS OF INLAY.

This type of rug-making is similar to the home craft of making rugs on canvas, but is more interesting and far more satisfying, since the maker of these rugs actually weaves the canvas and inserts the pile step by step.

For this rug the pile will be of rug wool and the background weft of string similar to that used for the warp. Weave first about four rows with string to give a firm edge. Now the first row of pile will be added using Ghiordes knot. The wool should first have been cut into pieces of equal length; about 2 inches is a useful size. Fold one of these lengths in two, and place the centre over the first two warp threads, starting from the left. Take the left-hand end round and under the first of these threads, and the right-hand end round and under the second one, bringing both ends out to the front below the band formed by the centre part of the thread. Then pull both ends tightly (Fig. 80a). Continue this process until a row of pile has been added. Then do two rows of weaving with string, beat up firmly, and add another row of pile. Warp ends of wool, cotton, etc., remaining on the loom after a piece of weaving has been completed can be cut up and used quite successfully for pile rugs.

G

Fig. 80a.—Ghiordes carpet knot.

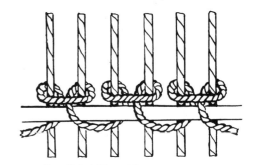

Fig. 80b.—Carpet knots over gauge.

If preferred the pile may be added as a continuous thread, instead of being first cut into lengths. For this purpose a gauge (a piece of wood of the required thickness with a groove along its length which enables the scissors to be slipped in the gauge easily when cutting the pile) is required, and the pile wool must be threaded into a sacking needle. Place the gauge across the warp. Starting from the right take the pile thread from front to back between the first and second warp threads, leaving a short end projecting in front. Take it under the first warp thread and out to the right, across the first two warp threads to the back, where it goes round and out to the front between these two threads below the loop it has made. Up to this point the gauge has not been used, but before starting the next loop the thread is now taken round this before passing between the next two warp threads (Fig. 80b). The above is perhaps the simplest form of carpet knot, but there are others, and also several different 'weaves' which may be used on such a loom. For these the reader must be referred to books dealing especially with the subject of carpet-weaving.

Woven and pile rugs may also be made on the Foot Power loom, and these will be much more quickly accomplished than on the small appliances already described. Unless the loom is very sturdy, the worker should not attempt rugs or runners of a greater width than 30 inches to 36 inches. The warp will be made in the same way as described for wool, a 4-ply wool, cotton or string carpet warp, and a single-ply or a 3- or 4-ply rug wool being used for weft, with a reed 10 or 12 dents to the inch. The entering would be 1, 2, 3, 4; repeat; heddles 1 and 3 and 2 and 4 being tied to each of two pedals. Only two heddles are really necessary, but if the loom is already equipped with four, they can be used as suggested to save dismantling the loom.

A great variety of striped rugs can be woven: the width and colours being varied to suit the individual taste. A good effect can be obtained by using two colours, one thread passing from the right and one from the left each time. This means that one colour will appear on the odd numbers in the warp, and the other on the even threads, resulting in equal perpendicular stripes of

84

FIG. 81.—RUGS WOVEN WITH STRIP FABRIC.

The warp was a flax twine and the colours of the strip fabric used in the weft were brown, fawn and heliotrope in the lower rug, and red and brown stripes on a yellow background in the upper one.

colour. The horizontal stripes will be produced by several rows of tabby weaving in one colour. It will be obvious that as all the warp must be covered, no special pattern rows, involving the passing over and under groups of threads, can be included, otherwise the raised warp strands would be left uncovered by the weft.

Pile rugs offer much more scope for variety in pattern. Each warp thread should pass through one dent of the reed (12 dents to the inch) except at the selvedge, where two threads should pass through each dent (three or four double threads should be allowed for the selvedge). A few inches of plain weaving should be done with the same material as used for the warp.

FIG. 82.—End of rug showing horizontal stripes produced by changing colour of weft.

85

A row of knots can now be made on each pair of warp strands—selvedge excepted. This means that, with 12 threads to the inch, there will be only six knots, and after each line of knots there must be two rows of tabby weaving in the foundation thread. The selvedge can be kept level by wrapping the weft in the form of a figure 8 round the warp strands, and so filling the gap left by the omission of the knots; the reed being used to beat up the rows as they are inserted. The colour of the pile can be changed as required, and in accordance with the pattern, which should be drafted before the work is started. The worker would be well advised to keep to fairly bold designs, as with so few knots to the inch it would be difficult to show any detailed pattern. The pattern can be drafted on squared paper—one square representing a knot; the number of knots being ascertained from the number of the warp threads—each knot requiring two warp strands.

This making of rugs is a very interesting branch of the weaver's craft, and with the choice of flat woven and pile rugs, with their different weaves and knots and their many possibilities for pattern design, it offers a very wide field for further practical experiment. Pile rugs can be woven on a foot-power loom of the Danish type (Fig. 119), while Fig. 73 shows a vertical Foot-Power Rug Loom.

Approximate Quantities of Materials required for the various looms :

	Small Frame For rug 40" x 17" WARP	Large Frame For rug 64" x 33" WARP	Large Loom For rug 84" x 31" WARP
Medium cotton yarn 8s/8 fold, used double	$\frac{1}{4}$ lb.	$\frac{3}{4}$ lb.	$1\frac{1}{4}$ lb.
Flax thread, used double	$\frac{1}{2}$ lb.	$1\frac{1}{2}$ lb.	$1\frac{3}{4}$ lb.
Thick cotton yarn 3s/18 fold, used single	$1\frac{1}{4}$ lb.	$3\frac{1}{2}$ lb.	$3\frac{3}{4}$ lb.
	WEFT	WEFT	WEFT
6-ply rug wool	$1\frac{3}{4}$ lb.	$4\frac{1}{4}$ lb.	$5\frac{3}{4}$ lb.

A weaver will realise that the amount of weft required will vary slightly in accordance with the tension of the weaving and that the approximate amount of both warp and weft required for rugs of other sizes can be calculated from the information given in the above table.

86

CHAPTER VIII
Longer Warps

THE weaving accomplished up to this point has been restricted, as was the work of the primitive weavers, to a length governed by the size of the loom. The weaver will now again experience the desire of her predecessors in wishing to produce longer pieces of fabric. Several primitive looms are shown in Figs. 50, 51, 52. In the case of the 'rigid-heddle' loom with a back strap described in Chapter VI, extra length became possible, since the long warp could be knotted at any point on the supporting hook. As the fabric grew it could be rolled on to its stick, and the warp could be untied and knotted farther away. Many primitive weavers adopted some such plan as this. The weaver sat on the ground with one end of the warp fixed to a stick which was tied round the waist, and the other end knotted round a peg stuck into the ground. An interesting primitive loom is depicted in Fig. 83; here the finished braid was rolled up, but the warp was knotted round a peg in the ground. When the weaving had proceeded almost as far as the heddles, the weaver had to leave it and walk a few yards in order to release more warp from the peg, then roll up the work and proceed with more weaving. The reader will notice that this loom also embodies the features mentioned in the previous chapter, viz., two heddles and a reed, but the former, instead of being *raised* by hand, are attached to rough pedals and *lowered* by means of the feet.

At what period the fairly obvious device was adopted of converting the cross beams of the early frame looms into rollers, it is impossible to say, but it has long been practised.

The weaver's problem now is to add the roller device to such looms as have already been used, so that a long warp may be rolled on at one end, and the cloth as it is woven rolled on at the other. The fixing of these rollers is an apparent difficulty, since there must be some arrangement to prevent them *unrolling* and so slackening the warp tension and making weaving impossible. This difficulty has led many weavers, at this stage, to buy ready-made looms, thus making their equipment expensive, but with the aid of a few useful tools it is easily overcome. The following are some possible methods:

I. Make a frame as in Fig. 63 in Chapter VI, or preferably the slightly stronger one in Fig. 84a, but for the lower strips substitute some 1-inch dowel rod A and B. The materials required will be: for the corner posts pieces of wood $\frac{5}{8}$ inch by $1\frac{1}{4}$ inches, and length according to height desired; for the rollers 1-inch dowel rod, length as required; for the top bars (above the

FIG. 83.—Horizontal narrow band loom, tripod form, from Tikonko, Mende, Sierra Leone (Bankfield Museum).

rollers) $\frac{1}{2}$-inch dowel rod, each piece to be $\frac{1}{2}$-inch longer than the rollers; all other parts $\frac{7}{8}$ inch by $\frac{5}{16}$ inch; in addition, four $\frac{1}{4}$-inch screw bolts 2 inches long with washers and wing nuts. The method of putting the side together is obvious, but note that the top pieces are placed *below* the *tops* of the corner posts, so as not to interfere with the shuttle in working, and that the oblique strengthening pieces must go in opposite directions on the two side pieces, to prevent the loom from buckling up under the strain of the warp. The position of the top rods must now be marked on the insides of the corner posts, and a cavity $\frac{1}{2}$ inch in diameter and $\frac{1}{4}$ inch deep to receive these is made with a brace and bit. The rollers must now be prepared to receive the screw bolt. To do this place the roller in a vice. Take a drill slightly smaller than the threaded part of the bolt, place it exactly in the centre of the end of the roller and drill a hole $\frac{1}{2}$ inch deep. This is done at each end of both rollers. A hole slightly larger than the bolt is made right through the corner posts at the points where the rollers are to fit. Now take the bolts with wing nuts and washers attached, insert them in the side posts, and screw well into the roller (Fig. 84*b*). The top bars are touched at the ends with glue, and inserted into their sockets before the rollers receive the final screwing.

It will now be found possible, by adjusting the wing nuts, to revolve the rollers, or to fix them at any desired point.

II. This is a development of the box used in the previous chapter. Wood of $\frac{5}{8}$ inch thickness will be required, together with some 1-inch dowel rod. The base of the box measures $9\frac{1}{2}$ by 18 inches, and may be of plywood or even of

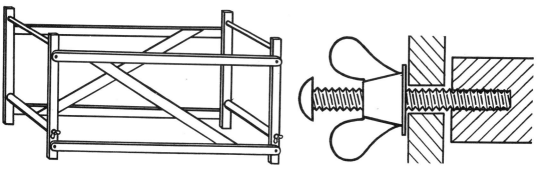

FIG 84a.—Simple loom with rollers.   FIG. 84b.—Detail of roller.

strawboard, as this base is not essential for strength, but will be useful for storing wool, shuttles, etc. The construction is obvious from Fig. 85. The side pieces measure 18 by 3 inches, and the ends $8\frac{1}{2}$ by $2\frac{1}{2}$ inches. Before fixing the parts it will be well to drill the holes which contain the rollers. These will be of 1 inch diameter, and made with a brace and bit right through the wood. Now, there is a choice of methods of fixing: (a) the rollers in this case are $\frac{1}{4}$ inch longer than the width of the loom. Nail with two or three small nails to each end of the rollers a circular disc of plywood $1\frac{1}{2}$ inches in diameter which has previously had a series of holes $\frac{1}{2}$ inch apart drilled just inside the circumference. Similar holes are drilled into the side of the box in such a position that a nail or peg may be inserted through a hole in the disc and into a hole in the

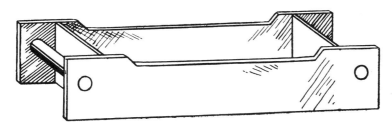

FIG. 85.—Simple box loom with rollers.

side of the box (Fig. 86a), thus preventing the roller from turning. (b) For this the roller should be of such length as to be flush with the outside of the loom on either side. Two holes are drilled diagonally right through the rollers, at the point where the roller will lie under the centre of the side piece of the box. A similar hole is drilled down the thickness of the box at this point, from the top to the opening for the roller. A nail or peg inserted into this hole will now fit into any one of four positions, and keep the roller fixed at that point (Fig. 86b). (c) The rollers should project 1 inch beyond the box on each side and holes should be drilled as in (b). Three nails are driven into the side of the loom as in

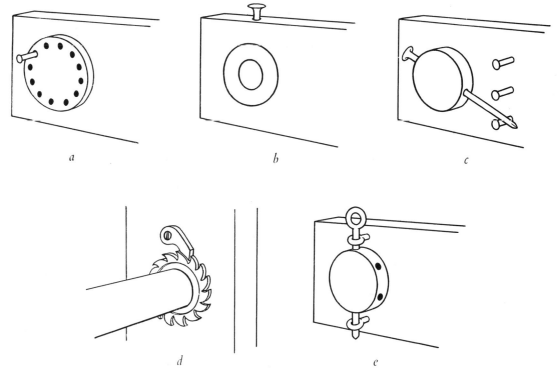

Figs. 86a, b, c, d, and e.—Various methods of fixing rollers.

illustration, and a long nail or peg inserted through the roller will be held against one of these and so fix the roller in position (Fig. 86c).

Either of the above looms may be fitted with the ratchet-and-pawl arrangement, which is customary in large hand looms, and which the reader may have used in tightening and fixing a tennis net. A small toothed wheel, the ratchet, is fixed on the end of the roller, and a movable catch, the pawl, is fixed on the frame of the loom in such a way that it can fall into a tooth of the ratchet and prevent it from revolving (Fig. 86d). Still another method may be adopted (Fig. 86e). Several holes are drilled right through the roller which projects a little beyond the frame of the loom; into this, above and below the roller are screwed ring head screws. A nail inserted into the ring passes through any one of the holes in the roller and holds this in position.

In order to facilitate the tying on of the warp, and to avoid waste of wool, each roller should be equipped with a piece of strong unbleached calico, which is nailed on to the roller and comes up to receive the warp. The width of this should be sufficient to go along practically the whole length of the rollers, and it should be from 9 inches long according to the size of the loom.

Before attaching it to the rollers turn down and stitch a hem a little wider than is necessary to receive a warp stick. Behind the stick, work a series of six eyelets $\frac{1}{4}$ inch in diameter, in the linen, at equal distances apart, the outer ones being 1 inch from the edges. Through these eyelets will pass strings attaching a further stick, on to which bunches of warp threads may be tied.

If the weaver prefers to buy such looms, similar ones to those illustrated in Figs. 63 and 84a can be purchased, also the sturdy Tabby Looms (Figs. 87 and 88) complete with rigid heddles to weave material of widths varying from $3\frac{1}{2}$ to 20 inches.

Now the loom is equipped with rollers, and the next problem to be dealt with is the making and putting on of the long warp. Hitherto it has been

FIG. 87.—Dryad Roller Loom with mounted heddle.

FIG. 88.—Dryad Tabby Loom.

a simple matter to wind the warp round and round the loom, or to cut a number of strands of equal length, since the lengths required have always been fairly short. But now the minimum requirement will be perhaps about 200 strands, each 2 yards long, and a hopeless tangle may be the result of an unguided effort to produce this. The beginner cannot hope to evolve a satisfactory method, but must be content to be told, and to admire the ingenuity of the minds who discovered it. Primitive weavers drove pegs into the ground, and carrying their warp thread along, walked round and round these pegs—no small task if a 40-yard warp of a few hundred strands had to be made! The attempt to avoid this lengthy task has led to the evolution of the *warping board*. This will be needed for later work on the table and large hand looms, and will therefore be

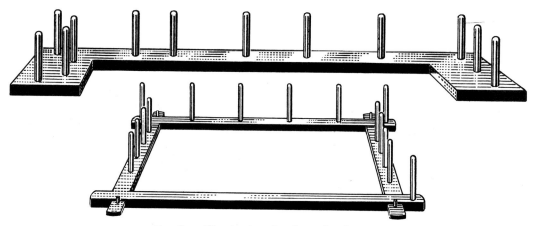

FIG. 89.—Warping board and warping frame.

described now; but if it cannot be obtained at this stage, the weaver must be content to modify it into the form of long nails driven into a board, using these by the method to be described for the warping board. Another alternative is to use a series of clamps with wooden uprights, such as are used for supporting a ping-pong net. These can be fixed to desks or tables as required, and may be purchased as single pegs, or in pairs (see Fig. 58), and a collection of these is more economical and far more useful than a warping board in classes where several pupils need to make warps at the same time. A warping frame, Fig. 90, can also be used for warps from 8 to 9 yards long, the pegs being arranged to give the necessary length of warp.

It will be noticed that the threads on the frame are crossed between pegs A

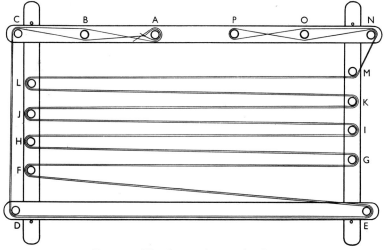

FIG. 90.—Warping on the warping frame.

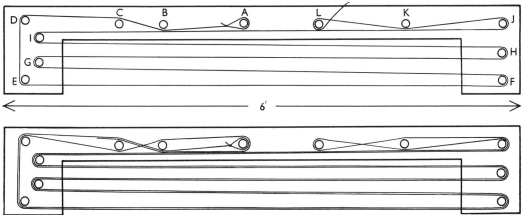

FIG. 91.—Warping on the warping board.

and B at one end and O and P at the other. (This cross applies to all warps whether made on posts, frame, board or mill.)

The warp starts at A, goes under B, round C, D, E, and so on until peg O is reached. The thread is then taken over O, under and round peg P, then under O, and so on till peg B is reached. The warp thread is then taken over peg B, under and round A, under B and so on throughout the warp.

For a shorter warp some of the pegs can be omitted, e.g. A to C, D, E, F, then up to peg L, M and finally to peg P.

The warping board is a much stronger piece of apparatus and is useful for longer warps. It has twelve pegs, each of which is removable to ease the strain on the warp when taking it from the board.

The warp should start at peg A, pass under B and over C, then round pegs D, E, F, G, H, I, J, under peg K, over and round peg L (Fig. 91).

For the return journey the warp should pass over peg K, round pegs J, I, etc., to peg D. Then under peg C, over peg B, over and round peg A, back under peg B and over peg C.

This procedure should be repeated throughout. It will be seen that the crosses appear between pegs B and C at one end and between pegs K and L at the other.

Before removing the warp from the board the crosses should be secured by passing a piece of string through the opening made by peg C and back through the opening made by peg B at one end and between L and K at the other end, and tying the string securely.

Another string should secure the threads at peg A.

Before using the board we must decide how many threads are required. A 15-inch scarf, having 14 threads to the inch, would require 210 threads, to which must be added 4, to give two double threads at each edge for a firm selvedge. Thus 214 threads are needed. An extra 9 inches to 12 inches must be added to the length required for the scarf—for tying on at the front of the loom and for wastage at the end of the warp. Two balls of wool will be required, and each must be put into a jar or box in which it can move freely, to prevent it from rolling about the floor. It is a great saving of time if a 'rice' or 'swift' is available, in which case the wool may be taken directly from the skeins to the warping board. Two threads will be warped at once, the weaver being careful to keep a forefinger always between the two to prevent crossing. Knot the two ends together, slip them over peg A, now carry both together under B, over C, and round the other pegs as indicated by the lines, Fig. 91, finishing under peg K and over and round L. Now return over K, round J, and retrace the path already taken and finish under C, over B, over and round peg A. Four threads have now been warped, and the same procedure is followed until there are 214 on the board. In order to avoid losing count it is well to put a tie of coloured wool round the group of strands, marking the count at regular intervals, i.e. every 14 strands, thus marking the number of inches of warp prepared—or every 20 or 50 as the weaver prefers.

The important feature of this method is the production of *crosses* by the alternation of the track of the warp, between pegs B and C, and L and K. If the warp is examined it will be seen that every pair of threads is by this means kept quite separate from its neighbours. This is of tremendous help in the threading up of the warp, and must be most carefully preserved. For this purpose a strand of coloured wool must be taken through the warp from front to back, through the opening made by peg C, and back through the opening made by peg B, and its ends knotted to form a long loop. Another front to back, through the opening made by peg A, should secure the threads at peg A. The cross between L and K is secured in the same way as that between B and C, Fig. 93.

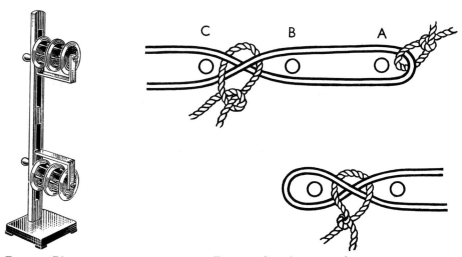

FIG. 92.—Rice.

FIG. 93.—Securing crosses in warp.

The warp is now ready to be taken off the board. To do this, push the right hand through the opening in the warp made by peg L. Now grasp the whole warp beyond K and draw it through the loop thus made. Continue this process, which is really a crochet chain with the hand as crochet hook (Fig. 94), until the warp is almost used up, and is ready to be put on the loom. Now take two flat shed sticks, with holes at each end. Insert one at each side of the adjoining cross (where the coloured threads lie).

Tie these two sticks together, through the hole at each end, to preserve the cross. The cord which was tied round the loops at A and through the crosses should now be removed.

FIG. 94.—Method of taking warp from the warping board.

These loops must now be put through the reed from front to back. (The reed, as mentioned on page 71, is the appliance which is used for keeping the warp threads evenly spaced and for beating up the rows of weft as they are inserted.) As this process is only for spacing or spreading out the warp, prior to winding the warp on the warp beam or roller, it is unnecessary to thread through each dent of the reed at this stage. Therefore, four threads or two loops are put through every fourth dent. When the single loop made at the beginning and end of the warp is reached, this should be put through with the two other loops, and the corresponding two dents allowed. It will be well if two people can work together at this stage. The person at the front of the loom should pass the loops, while the one at the back should pull them through the reed by means of a reed hook (Figs. 96*a* and 96*b*).

These loops are threaded on to another warp stick, to prevent them from slipping, or, if the warp is only a narrow one, the loops, as they are passed from the front of the loom, may be slipped in their right order on to a finger of the weaver at the back of the loom. These can be transferred to a stick later. It may be an advantage, especially for longer warps, to use the special non-slip knot (Fig. 127) when putting the loops of the warp (after passing through the reed) on the extra warp stick. This method eliminates the slipping of the threads when winding on the warp and avoids wastage of material because, when the warp threads are held tightly for winding on the back roller or warp beam, the

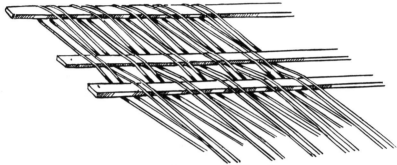

Fig. 95.—Cross in warp threads.

non-slip knot tightens the threads on the warp stick. It will be found that by this method, when the end of the warp is reached the threads are of a more even length. In threading these loops through the reed it is most important to keep them in their right order. If the person at the front of the loom pulls the warp taut the crosses will be obvious, and it will be noted that two threads go over and under the warp sticks alternately (Fig. 95).

When all the warp threads have been passed through the reed, and slipped on to a warp stick, this must be fastened to the stick running through the linen attached to the back roller, by tying with string through the eyelets in the linen.

The cross in the warp is still at the front of the loom, and it must now be transferred to the back. To do this the warp should be pulled taut at the front of the loom, and the string tying the ends of the two warp sticks together should now be cut.

The stick (now known as the 'shed stick') nearest the reed is placed on its edge near the reed, thus making a larger space between the top and bottom set of threads. A new stick is now put through the space or shed thus formed at the back of the reed, and the first stick removed. A string should be tied across the stick from one end to the other to avoid any risk of its slipping out, thereby

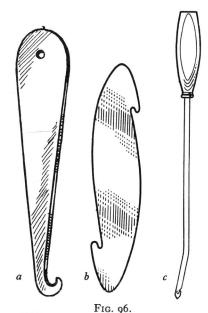

FIG. 96.

(*a* & *b*) Reed hooks. (*c*) Threading hook.

losing the cross. This stick should be pushed towards the warp beam.

The front shed stick should then be turned on edge, and the same process followed. The two shed sticks are now at the back of the reed, and should be kept near the reed during the winding on of the warp, otherwise they will wind on the roller with the warp. Some weavers prefer to leave the cross at the front of the loom until the warp has been wound on but the authors prefer the former method. One person should now wind the warp on to the back roller, the other should hold the warp tightly, half in one hand and half in the other.

The fingers should be used frequently as a comb to remove any tangles towards the end of the warp and away from the loom. It is essential that all threads should be kept at the same tension during this process, also that the selvedge threads at each side should be prevented from getting slack, as this would be a great handicap when weaving.

During the winding of the warp on to the warp beam, flat sticks (warp sticks) slightly longer than the width of warp should be placed round the roller at intervals. This prevents the various layers of warp threads from getting intermingled. Instead of sticks, sheets of clean paper may be rolled in between the layers of warp.

When practically the whole of the warp, with the exception of a few inches, has been wound on to the roller, the threads should be cut and pulled through the reed. Before doing this, however, the two 'shed sticks' should be tied at the back roller, for if this is omitted they are likely to fall when the threads are pulled through, and result in the cross, which the weaver has been at such pains to preserve, being lost. When the threads have been pulled through the reed, they should be tied in bunches in readiness for the 'threading-up' or 'entering' in the heddles. The heddles, as explained on page 70, are made of string with an eyelet in each, through which the warp strands pass. The heddles, when raised or lowered, produce the various patterns. This is done exactly as described in Chapter VI, the order of threading being very obvious owing to the way the warp is spread out on the sticks, and the threads separated by the cross. As the threading is done, the warp strands are knotted in small bundles of about 20 threads, in front of the reed, to prevent them from slipping back. It now remains only to attach the warp to the front roller. This is done as follows: having tied an additional warp stick to the end of the linen, as previously described, take a bunch of threads from the right of the warp, untie it, pass it from the underside of this stick up through the space between the two sticks. Take the right-hand half of the bunch, pass it over the stick to the right and, under the whole bunch of threads to the left. Take the left-hand half in the opposite direction (see Fig. 97). Tie the two halves together in a single knot across the bunch. Repeat this process next with the left-hand bunch of threads, and then with the others in turn.

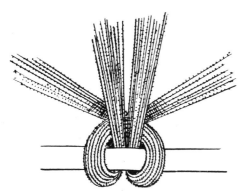

FIG. 97.—Method of attaching warp to front roller.

It is now necessary to look over the warp to see that the tension is uniform, and that there are no loose threads. Any necessary adjustments having been made, a final knot is made in the ends of each bunch. The beginner must not be afraid of having a tightly stretched warp, as a slack one makes it very difficult to obtain a good shed.

Before an actual piece of work is begun, a few rows of weaving in any oddments of wool should be done in order to draw the warp together, and to show any mistakes which may have been made in threading. It is wise to insert a warp stick in each shed before starting to weave, as this helps the beating up of the first few throws of weft.

To make a Cotton Warp.—If only a short warp is needed, the warping board described in Chapter VIII can still be used, but for a very long warp a warping mill will be necessary (Fig. 98). This is a much larger piece of apparatus, consisting of a skeleton reel, which turns freely on a metal rod fitted into a socket in the base. It consists of four uprights and two cross-pieces of wood, one of these being fitted with three pegs to correspond with A, B, C on the warping board, the other with three pegs which correspond with J, K and L on the board. The four uprights are bored with a series of holes from the top to the bottom, so that the cross-bars can be fixed at any height desired, this depending on the length of warp to be made. If the distance between the uprights is 27 inches, the total circumference will be 3 yards. It is therefore a simple matter to make a warp of any length. A warp 12 yards long would mean four times round the mill.

The method of warping on the mill is similar to that of the board (see Fig. 91), starting at top left-hand peg A and round to finishing point L. The threads are guided on their way by the weaver's left hand, the mill being turned with the right while the weaver remains stationary.

98

FIG. 98.—Warping mill.

FIG. 99.—Spool rack.

If a fine warp is required, e.g., one in mercerised cotton, it is obvious that if only two threads are warped at a time, the process will be a slow one. By means of a spool rack (Fig. 99) a number of threads can be warped simultaneously. Eight or ten threads would be a convenient number, two spools being put on each bar of the rack. Thus, if eight threads were taken from A to L and back to A, sixteen threads would have been warped. When making a fine warp, it is most essential to keep the crosses between the pegs in single, rather than double, threads. To do this, first tie the eight threads together, and slip half on top and half underneath peg A. The cross must now be made with the thumb and first finger. This is done by placing the right thumb over the lowest thread nearest to the weaver, the first finger over the other thread of this lowest pair. This means that the first thread taken is under the thumb and over the first finger, the second thread is over the thumb and under the first finger (Fig. 100). The second pair of threads is taken in a similar way, and so on until eight threads are alternately over the thumb and under the first finger, when the cross between these threads will be obvious. The cross must now be transferred to the pegs A, B, C, so that the cross is between pegs B and C. The eight

H

99

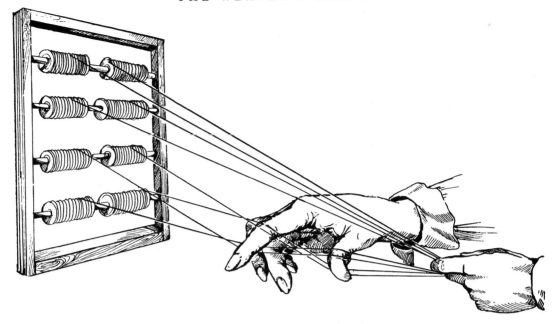

FIG. 100.—Method of crossing threads.

threads are now carried in ONE BUNCH round the mill, round peg J, under peg K, over and round peg L. For the return journey the warp should pass (as previously described) over peg K, round peg J and back to peg C, where the threads should again be crossed singly with the finger and thumb and transferred to pegs B and C. This process should be repeated throughout the warp, with the crosses between pegs B and C and K and L each time. The threads should be tied either in inches: i.e., if the material to be woven is 28 threads to the inch (a suitable number for cotton), the warp threads could be tied in bunches of 28; if the material is 30 inches wide, it will need 30 bunches; or, if preferred, the warp threads can be tied up in patterns; i.e., if 26 threads to a pattern, and 11 patterns across the width, the threads would be tied in 11 bunches of 26 threads; but the former method is more satisfactory, for reasons which will be described later. The crosses must be secured between pegs C and B and K and L, and this done, the warp can now be taken from the mill, beginning at peg A (not at L as for a wool warp), and made into a chain in the same way as a wool warp.

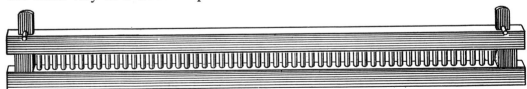

FIG. 101.—Raddle or spreader.

The warp is now ready to be wound on to the warp beam—to do this the loop taken from peg L must be attached to the warp beam. This 30 inches of warp must now be spread evenly across the warp beam. For this purpose a raddle or spreader is necessary (Fig. 101). This consists of a wooden comb with a movable top to cover the ends of the teeth, and should be tied to the uprights of the loom in line with the warp beam, the top removed, and the threads placed in the dents. The raddle can have a varying number of evenly spaced teeth or dents—two or more—to the inch. Therefore, if a raddle with two dents per inch is used for 30 inch material for which the warp has been tied up in inches, half of one of these bunches of threads could be placed in each dent. The thread tying each inch can be unfastened as required, when the placing of each ½ inch in a dent will be a simple matter. When the warp has thus been spread across the raddle, the top of the latter should be fixed on by means of the two pegs—the warp is then ready for winding on the beam. Two people must work together for this process, one to free the warp from any tangles, the other to wind the threads on to the warp beam—inserting warp sticks at intervals.

When warping several threads together of different colour or thickness it is advisable to use more threads than the number of shafts (heddle frames) on the loom e.g. a warp could be made of six threads, the fifth being a thick cotton or gimp, the others of fine cotton. Two spools should be put on each bar of the spool rack. In threading a four shaft loom, the thick (5th) thread will come alternately on the first and third shaft—thus giving a more interesting effect to the fabric.

Cotton and silk are more liable to become tangled than wool, and to free the warp from these tangles the worker should, with a soft clothes brush, draw any loose threads away from the loom and towards the end of the chain. Some weavers find it satisfactory merely to shake the warp in order to free it from tangles. The person holding the warp should keep the threads at as even a tension as possible, paying special attention to the selvedge threads. The chain unravels as the warp is wound on the beam, and this winding should be continued until the other end of the warp is reached. The cross so carefully guarded at B and C, is now reached, and shed sticks should be inserted between B and C, the ends being tied together to avoid the risk of the sticks slipping out. The raddle can now be removed, and the sticks preserving the cross can be moved towards, and tied to, the warp beam. The loops at the end of the warp can now be cut and tied in bunches ready for 'entering'.

The process is now similar to that followed for a wool warp. The texture of the material or number of dents to the inch becomes a matter for experience; some hints were given in the previous chapter, and much may be learned as the result of experiment.

CHAPTER IX
Simple Four-Heddle Box Loom

UP to this point only two heddles have been used for the plain or tabby weaving; and pattern has been achieved either by coloured bands in weft only or in warp or weft, or by darning with needle or shuttle under and over groups of threads (see Chapter III).

Having invented labour-saving devices for the plain weaving, the weaver was at first content to work in pattern by the more laborious method, but the human mind is always active, especially where time and labour may be saved as a result of thought; hence came the suggestion of the possibility of developing the heddle arrangement for use in pattern weaving.

The weaver will no doubt experiment with the simple box loom referred to in the previous chapter (Fig. 85). This had two rollers and two heddles, but will now have an additional pair of heddles for the purpose of pattern-weaving (see Fig. 102). A slightly different construction is suggested from that referred to above. It has been altered to avoid the difficulty experienced by amateurs in producing the 'cut-away' side of the previous model. The various pieces required may, if desired, be procured ready cut to size and are quite easy to assemble. They are as follows:

A. 2 pieces $7\frac{1}{2}$ in. $\times$ $3\frac{1}{2}$ in. $\times$ $\frac{5}{8}$ in.
B. 2   ,,   17 in. $\times$ $1\frac{1}{2}$ in. $\times$ $\frac{5}{8}$ in.
C. 4   ,,   4 in. $\times$ $3\frac{1}{2}$ in. $\times$ $\frac{5}{8}$ in.
D. 2   ,,   1 in. dowel rod $8\frac{1}{2}$ in. long.

Strawboard or plywood to fit base.

For Heddles. 5 mm. plywood.
8 strips $\frac{5}{8}$ in. $\times$ 8 in.
8   ,, $\frac{5}{8}$ in. $\times$ $6\frac{1}{2}$ in.

1 reed. 14 dents to 1 in. 100 dents wide (7 in. approx.).

The method of construction is much the same as that described for Loom II, Chapter VIII, with the following differences:

(1) The holes for rollers are made in each of the pieces marked C. All the parts should be temporarily placed in position, when it will be obvious that the rollers must be so placed as not to foul any of the adjacent parts.

(2) Two of the 'C' parts are then nailed or screwed in place on each of the 'A' pieces.

(3) The sides 'B' are now attached. The rollers may be controlled by any of the methods previously described. In this model, method *b* (Fig. 86), has been adopted.

FIG. 102.—FOUR-HEDDLE BOX LOOM.

(4) One hundred heddle strings should be made and four heddle frames (see Fig. 64). The frames, however, should not be closed up for the present, as the number of strings required on each frame will vary according to the pattern chosen and if they are fastened now the heddle strings cannot be slipped on.

The width of the warp must of course be decided upon beforehand. For the purpose of this loom a simple 'thread up' or form of 'entering' will be chosen, i.e., one of eight threads only. Therefore, if the fabric is to be of such width as to need twelve patterns, there must be ninety-six threads.

To these must be added four extra threads for the selvedge at either side, making a total of one hundred and four. There will be 14 threads to the inch (the number generally used for scarves, etc.), so it will be seen that the warp will be about 7 inches wide. From this 7-inch strip of woven material such things as small needle cases, pochettes, trimmings, etc. can be made, as on the looms previously described.

Prior to this stage the threading up has been fairly simple: one warp thread passing through the first heddle on No. 1 frame, the next through the first heddle on the second frame, and so on. Each heddle was lifted up or pulled down to make the alternate 'sheds' through which the weft thread passed. On the box loom the heddles can only be lifted, and the resulting patterns are in accordance with the order in which this is done. There are various simple ways of threading up or entering, and the order in which the warp threads are entered into the heddles will determine the variety and type of patterns that can be produced.

Pattern-making is dealt with more fully in connection with the table and foot-power looms. It will suffice here to explain one simple entering with which the weaver can experiment, and so gain experience and an understanding of the principles underlying the making of patterns, which will be of considerable help in working on the table loom (the principles of which are precisely the same as those used in the simple box loom). The four heddles should be placed in the box, and numbered, to avoid any mistake, 1, 2, 3, 4, from the front to the back of the loom. This means that heddle No. 1 will be nearest to the weaver, No. 4 will be nearest to the warp roller.

Some writers, in referring to table looms, etc., suggest numbering the heddle frames 1 to 4 from back to front of the loom; but as the method of numbering usually adopted in the hand loom is 1 to 4 from front to back of the loom, the writers adopt this method throughout in order to avoid confusion later.

One of the simplest methods of entering is 1, 2, 3, 4, which means that the first thread passes through the first heddle on No. 1 frame, the second through the first heddle on No. 2 frame, the third through the first heddle on No. 3 frame, and the fourth through the first heddle on No. 4 frame. This is repeated, and the first thread of the second pattern will pass through the second heddle on heddle frame No. 1, and so on until all threads are entered. Each heddle frame raises one thread in every four, and if the four heddles are lifted consecutively, threads Nos. 1, 2, 3, 4 will be lifted in that order. This thread up is used for twills (referred to in a previous chapter), and only gives a limited number of patterns.

In order to give a little more scope the following 'diamond' thread up is chosen, and by means of pattern drafts, photographs, etc., some of the many patterns that can be achieved are illustrated. The order of entering is as follows : 2, 3, 4, 1, 4, 3, 2, 1. As pattern drafts are always read from right to left, the figures are given in the same order as the pattern drafts will appear, and should *therefore be read from right to left*. For entering it is an advantage if two persons can work together—one to sort out the threads at the cross, putting them in their right order, the other to pull each thread in turn through the correct heddle.

It is quite possible, though a considerably slower process, for one person to do the entering, but the former method is recommended and described. The person behind the warp roller should sit at the left of the loom (looking at the loom from the back), and should sort out the first four threads which will make the selvedge at this side. These should be taken in order, and threaded by means of a reed hook (this can be made quite satisfactorily from a piece of spring steel, see Fig. 96*b*), through heddles 4, 3, 2, 1, for selvedge. This means that the first thread will pass through the first heddle on heddle frame No. 1, the second through the first heddle on heddle frame No. 2, and so on until the four threads for selvedge are entered and the pattern itself reached. These four selvedge threads should be tied in a bunch. The eight pattern threads should be entered in their order, 2, 3, 4, 1, 4, 3, 2, 1, and when completed checked and tied in a bunch.

This process should be repeated until the last four threads are reached, and these should then be entered through heddles 4, 3, 2, 1, in a similar way to that adopted for the first selvedge. The entering of the heddles is now complete. As 14 threads to the inch were allowed when making the warp, a reed with 14 dents to the inch will be needed.

Threading the Reed.—The threads, having been drawn through the heddles, are ready to enter the reed in their regular order, starting at the same end from which the entering was done; the first two selvedge threads are passed through the first dent of the reed, the second pair of selvedge threads through the second dent. After this only one thread should pass through each dent until the second selvedge is reached, care being taken to avoid missing a dent or passing two pattern threads through a dent. As each set of eight threads is entered, it should be tied in a bunch in front of the reed. When the second selvedge is reached two double threads should be passed through each of the last two dents of the reed. If two people work together for the threading up, the warp threads can be passed through the heddles, and then through the dents of the reed at one operation. When all threads have been passed through the reed, and tied in bunches at the front, they must next be tied to the front roller in the way described in Chapter VIII.

When all are tied in this way, check the threading and test the tension with the fingers. All threads should be firm and springy, so any loose ones should be re-tied. This complete, another knot should be tied to make the ends more secure, and all is ready for weaving.

Before beginning to weave, a stick should be inserted in each shed, then the weft wool must be wound evenly on the shuttles. If the weaving is all in one colour, only one shuttle will be necessary. Two shuttles will, however, be required—one for the plain weaving, or binder (that is, the plain row of weaving which comes between each pattern row), and one for the pattern weaving, when the latter is in a contrasting colour to the groundwork. If this binder is not used between the pattern rows, the weaving tends to become rather loose, especially if more than three or four pattern rows are worked over any group of warp threads.

If heddles Nos. 1 and 3 are now lifted together, it will be seen that one set of alternate threads is raised. This points to the necessity for lifting Nos. 1 and 3 and 2 and 4 alternately for plain weaving (see pattern draft No. 1, Fig. 103). When lifting two heddle frames together the weaver will find it an advantage to slip a piece of wood, a few inches long, under the two frames, while passing the shuttle through the shed. This strip of wood will then rest on the two heddles which have not been lifted. A few rows of plain weaving should be done, and then it would be well for the worker to experiment by lifting the heddles in different combinations, and putting a thread through the 'shed'. This should be in a contrasting colour to the warp, so that the pattern shows more clearly. It will be found after experimenting that the order of lifting the heddles can be varied as follows:

(1) Each heddle can be lifted singly, giving certain threads up or down (this can be tested by the weaver) (see drafts 2 and 3).

(2) Two heddles can be lifted together, Nos. 1 and 3 and 2 and 4 for plain weave; Nos. 1 and 2, 1 and 4, 3 and 4, 2 and 3 for pattern-weaving.

A great variety of patterns can be produced by lifting the heddles in any of the above combinations, and the length of the pattern can be extended by putting a number of rows through any one shed, e.g. four rows through the shed made by lifting Nos. 1 and 4, with a plain row between each. When weaving with a pattern thread and a binder, the threads should be locked at the selvedge by passing the thread to be used round the one just used. For plain weaving a definite plan of passing the shuttle through the shed should be decided upon to avoid confusion, e.g. from right to left, when lifting heddles Nos. 1 and 3, and from left to right with heddles Nos. 2 and 4. When experienced, weavers can adapt the methods described to suit their own individual ideas and needs. In fact, stress should be laid on *experiment* and *individuality* throughout a weaving course.

The weaver will now realise that patterns can be woven by this method far more expeditiously than by the 'darning-in' method mentioned in earlier chapters. Later, she will again realise that the results on the more advanced table loom are obtained more quickly than on the simple box loom. The reader will easily realise that for the purpose of pattern-weaving the board loom previously used may now be equipped with four sets of leashes. The principles of pattern-weaving may easily be demonstrated on such a loom but it is less easily manipulated than the one just described (see Fig. 105).

It seems advisable at this stage to introduce simple pattern drafts so that the weaver can realise beforehand the type of patterns that can be achieved from a particular thread up. Squared paper will be used; one row of horizontal

"Diamond" Threading Draft

Read from Right to Left.

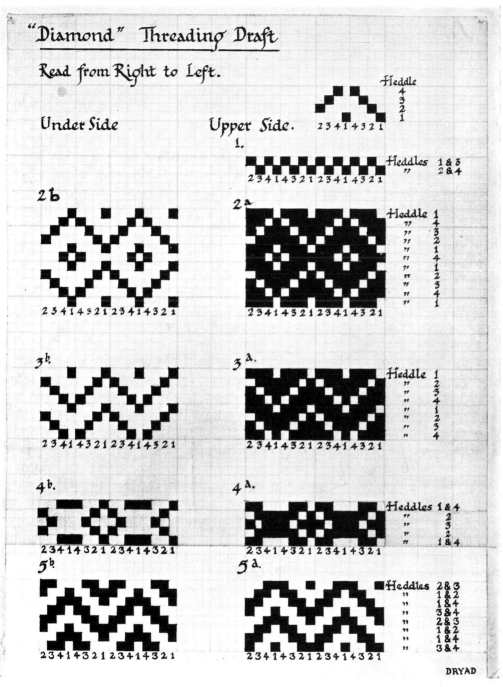

Under Side.　　　Upper Side.

FIG. 103.

squares will represent one row of weft, whilst one row of vertical squares represents one warp thread. The pattern will be indicated by filling in the squares which will be covered by the weft. Four rows of horizontal squares should be ruled off across the top of the draft to represent the heddles, and these should be numbered from top to bottom 4, 3, 2, 1, on the right-hand side, No. 1 being the first heddle at the front of the loom. The selvedge can be ignored at this stage, the pattern only being drafted. On the four rows of squares the threading should be marked (see threading draft, Fig. 103).

Underneath this the patterns should be drafted. If the heddles are lifted in the following order, 1, 4, 3, 2, 1, 4, 1, 2, 3, 4, 1, the pattern draft will appear as shown in diagrams 2a and 2b in Fig. 103, showing respectively the upper and under sides of the weaving. Compare this with the woven borders on Figs. 104a and 104b. It will be realised that the upper and lower sides of the weaving will be different, as the weft threads pass over a group on the upper side but under the same group on the under side of the work.

It will be seen that in the bottom line of the pattern draft all the threads going through the heddles on No. 1 frame are blocked in (this is the under side of the weaving, the progress of which can be watched with a mirror in the box loom).

As all the threads on No. 1 heddle are to be lifted, the weft thread will go under these, and over the remaining groups (see diagram 2a, Fig. 103). Looking at the draft again it will be seen that when heddle No. 4 is lifted, all threads on that frame are lifted (see diagram of upper side). The same idea can be followed throughout the draft, i.e. whenever a heddle is lifted the threads on that heddle are lifted, and the weft thread, in consequence, passes over the threads left down.

Diagram 3, Fig. 103, shows the pattern which can be woven by lifting heddles in the order 1, 2, 3, 4, 1, 2, 3, 4, then repeat. Two repeats of the pattern are drafted and one row of pattern on each heddle; but two more rows can be woven if preferred, which will, of course, tend to elongate the pattern.

The borders shown in Fig. 103 have been woven on a small box loom, and photographed as Figs. 104a and 104b, the only difference between the actual weaving and the draft being that two rows were woven to each change of heddle, whilst for convenience only one row is shown in the draft. It will be seen that in patterns 5a and 5b two heddles have, in some cases, been lifted together and that the patterns are reversed on upper and lower surfaces. Referring to Draft 5a, Fig. 103: if heddles 3 and 4 are raised then all threads on these heddles will be raised and the weft thread will pass over all the other warp strands.

A weaver should mark on squared paper the bottom row of the pattern—i.e. fill in all squares on heddles 1 and 2 as these are left down.

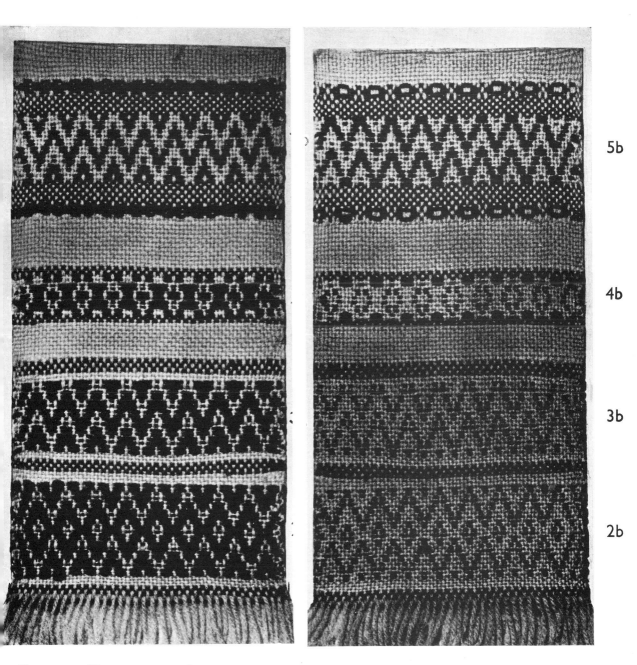

5b

4b

3b

2b

FIG. 104a.—UPPER SIDE OF A SAMPLER WOVEN
ON A FOUR-HEDDLE BOX LOOM.

FIG. 104b.—UNDER SIDE OF A SAMPLER WOVEN
ON A FOUR-HEDDLE BOX LOOM.

FIG. 105.—BOARD LOOM WITH FOUR LEASHES.

In the second row, as heddles 1 and 4 are raised all squares representing threads 2 and 3 are filled in.

In the third row, heddles 1 and 2 are raised, so squares representing threads 3 and 4 should be filled in.

In the fourth row, heddles 2 and 3 are raised, so threads 1 and 4 should be filled in on the pattern draft.

These four rows are then repeated as indicated on the draft.

It must be remembered that this draft appears on the upper side of the weaving and is the opposite of draft 5b, where the one pattern is white, the other is black, and vice versa. (On looking at a woven pattern with half-closed eyes, a weaver can get a faint impression of the pattern reproduced on the other side.) Reference is made to this reversing of the patterns, because in most of the small table looms the heddles are lifted, whilst in the foot-power loom they are lowered by means of pedals. Thus the pattern obtained on the under side of a table loom, in which the heddles are raised, will come on top of weaving on a pedal loom. But it should be quite easy to draft the patterns for either, after experimenting and understanding the small drafts given in this chapter. If, however, a weaver prefers to weave a pattern as indicated at 5*b*, but this to be on the upper side of the work, she can easily do so by altering the heddles indicated at the side of the draft. In the bottom row of the draft heddles 3 and 4 are indicated and so should be changed to 1 and 2. The list of heddles should read 1 and 2; 2 and 3; 3 and 4; 1 and 4. Repeat to the end of the pattern.

Other patterns can be drafted and woven, and there is great scope for experimenting even with this small loom, and from it a weaver can glean all the working principles of any four-heddle table or hand loom. Further pattern drafts will be given in connection with the table and foot-power looms. To get the best effect of a woven or drafted pattern it is advisable to look at it from a distance, also to draft the pattern fully, showing exact number of rows, etc., before actually weaving it. The weaving shown on the box loom, Fig. 102, was done from a portion of the Cleveland Web Threading Draft No. 12. This will now be given and should read from R. to L.

$$\underbrace{(12341234)}_{\text{Selvedge}}\ 12121\ \underbrace{(43434141232321414 34341\quad 2121)}_{\text{3 times}}\ \underbrace{(43214321)}_{\text{Selvedge}}$$

Other simple threading drafts useful for experiments are given in Chapter XII.

CHAPTER X
The Table Loom

HAVING had experience with various types of small looms and home-made appliances for making patterns, the weaver should now be ready for the table loom. This differs very little from the four-heddle loom dealt with in the previous chapter, as the working principles of the two looms are practically identical. The table loom, however, is larger and sturdier, and in consequence offers scope for the weaving of wide material suitable for table runners, cushions, scarves, garments, etc.

There are many useful table looms on the market with devices for the lifting or lowering of the heddles. Some of these are illustrated in Figs. 106–109. In addition, to the ingenious the construction of a table loom in the school or home is a simple matter. The main thing to be considered before starting to construct such a loom is the lifting device for the heddles.

Many original methods have been adopted for this, i.e. a leather strap or a piece of brass chain working through a slot in the top cross beam and fastening to a hook to hold the heddle frame stationary, whilst the shuttle is thrown. Various other practical ideas will occur to the weaver. Before leaving the subject of the heddles it may be as well to mention that in practice it is found that the heddle frames will need either a weight or a spring to bring them back to their original position after being lifted.

The other great point for the designer to consider is the method of fixing the rollers (warp and cloth beam) to prevent them from slipping whilst working. Several methods have been dealt with in a previous chapter: others may occur to the weaver; but the most usual method adopted in the table loom is a toothed ratchet wheel and catch.

The table loom does practically the same work as a large pedal loom, but on a smaller scale, and owing to the more convenient size and lower cost of the table loom, it is within the reach of many more people who are interested in the craft of weaving. The construction of the table loom is much simpler than that of the large pedal loom, though the working principles

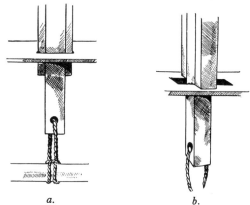

a.   b.

FIG. 106.—Lifting device for heddles.

are similar; the main differ-ence between the two looms being the method of working the heddles. In the latter type of loom the heddles are attached to treadles, each of which, when depressed by the foot, pulls down the corresponding heddle.

Generally speaking, the heddles in table looms are lifted, though some models have levers at the side to which the heddles are attached, and which, when pressed, pull down the corresponding heddle frame.

Figs. 107, 108, and 109

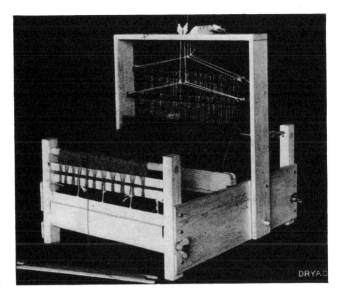

FIG. 107.—Dryad 'Wendy' Loom.

show three types of table looms. Though these differ in some details, the general working construction and working principles are the same. The principal parts of each loom are as follows:

A. Front Roller or Cloth Beam.
B. Back Roller or Warp Beam.
C. Heddles These are made of wire or string with a hole in the centre of each, through which the warp threads pass. There are four sets of heddles to each loom (i.e., to each four-way loom), each set being mounted on metal rods or a frame, and suspended from the top of the loom.
D. Reed and Batten used for regulating the warp threads and beating up the weft.
E. Shed Sticks, two smooth sticks with holes at the ends, used for pre-serving the cross in the warp.

The Warp.—The actual making of the warp has been dealt with in Chapter VIII, but as the transference of the warp to the table loom is a little more complicated than the method adopted for the smaller braid looms, etc., this will now be dealt with fully.

For a scarf or table runner approximately 14 inches wide and with 14 threads to the inch, we should need approximately 196 warp threads. The exact num-ber will be decided by taking the nearest multiple of the number of threads forming the required pattern. For instance, the Rosepath pattern uses eight threads; twenty-four complete patterns would need 192 threads. To this

FIG. 108.—Dryad 'Cottage' Loom.

number we add 16 threads, which are necessary to give a selvedge composed of four double threads at either edge. These are threaded singly through each heddle and double through the first four and last four dents of the reed. We need therefore a warp of 208 threads. An extra 12 inches to 18 inches should be added to the length of warp required for the scarf.

Materials for Use

1. Two- or three-ply warp wool.
2. Two- or three-ply weft wool (this is generally more loosely spun than the warp wool, but warp wool can be used for both warp and weft if preferred).
3. Cotton, mercerised cotton, gimp, chenille and other fancy yarns for more advanced work.
4. Reed.—For wool, 12-18 dents to 1 inch.
    For cotton, 24-26 dents to 1 inch, according to thickness of cotton.
    Instead of a reed with 24 dents, one with 12 dents could be used, putting two threads through each dent.

For this particular warp 3-ply orange wool was used. A warp 6 yards long and sufficient for three scarves or runners took 6 oz. of wool. (The weft should take approximately the same amount.)

114

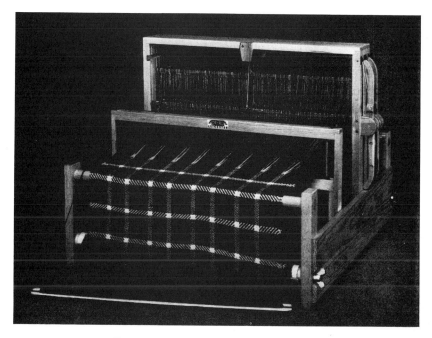

FIG. 109.—Dryad 'Wendicote' Table Loom.

Putting the Warp on the Loom.—The warp threads have been passed through the reed for spacing as previously described, and the remainder of the warp is at present in the form of a chain. This has now to be transferred to the warp beam. If two people work together the process is greatly simplified, and it can be carried out much more expeditiously. First decide on the number of heddles required on each heddle frame. As there are 208 threads in the warp, 208 heddles will be necessary.

On reading the Rosepath Threading Draft (Fig. 114), it will be seen that the eight pattern threads are equally divided between the four heddle frames, and in consequence, fifty-two heddles will be required on each frame.

The heddle frames on the Wendy Loom (Fig. 107) will not be fixed into position until after the warp has been wound on to the warp beam.

In the Wendicote Loom it will be necessary to remove the heddle frames from the loom before winding on the warp. To do this, raise the frames to the level of the grooves in the canopy and slide out. If extra heddles are necessary, these can be added by unscrewing the sides of the frame.

In the Cottage Loom, the heddle frames can be removed in a similar way by raising them to the level of the grooves in the canopy and sliding out. If extra heddles are required, the end of the frames should be unscrewed and the metal

I

weight at each end of the frame unhooked, when the extra heddles can be slipped on to the metal bars. This loom can easily be adapted to foot power by the addition of a stand which can be supplied separately.

Threading the Loom.—It is still an advantage for two people to work together for this, as the threads can be drawn through the heddles and reed simultaneously, thus lessening the chance of any error being made and saving a great deal of time. Fix heddle frames into position. The analysis of pattern will be dealt with more fully in another chapter. At this stage it will be better to get some idea of the working of the loom. This will be threaded up to the Rosepath pattern as follows: 1, 4, 3, 2, 1, 2, 3, 4. Other suitable threading drafts will be given; but the 'Rosepath' entering offers plenty of scope for experimenting and a great variety of patterns.

For the threading up, one person should sit at the back of the loom in such a position that the shed sticks and warp threads can be easily seen, as it is most essential that the latter should be entered in their correct order. The second person should sit at the front of the loom, and be ready to pull the threads through the heddle and reed. The heddle frames are numbered 1, 2, 3, 4, from front to back of the loom. The threading draft 1, 4, 3, 2, 1, 2, 3, 4, should be read from right to left, and the actual threading up should be started at the right of the loom (looking at the front).

When making the warp, four double threads were allowed for each selvedge, and the right selvedge must be entered first, through heddles 1, 2, 3, 4, 1, 2, 3, 4, reading from right to left. The person at the back of the loom should find the first thread and pass it through the first heddle on frame No. 4; the second through the first heddle on frame No. 3; the third through the first heddle on frame No. 2; the fourth through the first heddle on frame No. 1; the fifth through the second heddle on frame No. 4; the sixth, seventh, and eighth through the second heddle on each of the frames Nos. 3, 2, 1. This completes the selvedge, and these threads should now be drawn through the reed. Selvedges can be threaded in one of two ways: either singly through the heddles and double through the reed or double through heddles and reed. This should be a matter of choice for the weaver. The position in the reed must be measured accurately. The reed is 21 inches long, the warp 14 inches wide; therefore, $3\frac{1}{2}$ inches must be left at each end of the reed.

The first pair of selvedge threads should thus enter a dent of the reed $3\frac{1}{2}$ inches from the end, the next pair through the next dent, and so on.

Now the actual pattern must be threaded, putting each thread through one heddle and one dent of the reed. Only one thread of each pair must now be taken at a time from the back roller, and care must be taken to prevent the heddles themselves, particularly the string or cotton type, from getting crossed.

As each pattern is threaded up it should be checked and tied in a bunch at the front of the loom to prevent the threads from slipping through the reed again. A weaver may find it an advantage, especially when threading up one of the longer drafts, to indicate the end of *each* pattern by tying a string temporarily through the reed. This will simplify the checking of the patterns as the weaver can see at once at which point in the reed each new pattern commences. Any errors in the threading should be rectified and the strings which were put through the reeds should then be removed. The importance of checking the number of threads and the 'entering' of each pattern cannot be stressed too strongly.

One mistake in the threading up, particularly of the more complicated patterns given later on, may mean the re-entering of the whole warp. It is easy to check patterns if the person at the front pulls her bunch of threads taut.

All the threads should be put through heddles and reed in their right order, until the last eight threads for the second selvedge are reached.

As the last pattern thread passes through No. 1 heddle, the first selvedge thread passes through No. 4. It is usual to reverse the order of threading the second selvedge but this can only be done if it fits in with the last pattern thread. The selvedge in this case could be threaded in one of two ways, either 1, 2, 3, 4, or 1, 4, 3, 2 (reading from right to left).

The first selvedge thread cannot pass through heddle No. 1 as two adjacent threads would in that case be pulled down together and thus disturb the tabby weave.

The entering is now complete, and the threads have only to be tied on to the front roller in the same way as described for the box loom. As there are eight threads to a pattern it is advisable to tie the threads on to the front shed stick in pattern groups of eight threads. This will greatly simplify the checking up (particularly in the case of patterns with a larger number of threads, e.g. Honeysuckle) if a mistake has been made in the entering of the threads in the heddles. The level of the heddle frames must then be tested, and should be such that the warp threads, in passing through the centre of the heddle eyes from the back to the front roller, remain horizontal. Any adjustment can be made by altering the length of the string. The simplest way of attaching the string to the frames is as follows: first put a knot in the end of the string hanging from the cross beam (the height of this knot can be altered to suit each frame). The string is then passed under the heddle frame and the short end tied round the long piece, which is pulled tight: the knot prevents the short end of the string from slipping through, and holds the frame quite securely (Fig. 110). In the Wendy Loom a string will have to be threaded through the hole in one end of the heddle frame and stretched to the other end and tied. An extra piece of string will be attached to this after passing through the hole in the top cross bar.

As the string stretches during the weaving it can readily be adjusted at this small knot. It will be well at first for the weaver to experiment with the lifting of various heddles, and see the resulting pattern rows. In the same way as with the four-heddle box loom, it will be found that the heddles can be lifted in the following combinations:

FIG. 110.—Knot for attaching heddles.

$$\left.\begin{array}{l} \text{1 and 3} \\ \text{2 and 4} \end{array}\right\} \text{Plain}$$

$$\left.\begin{array}{l} \text{1 and 2} \\ \text{2 and 3} \\ \text{3 and 4} \\ \text{1 and 4} \end{array}\right\} \text{Pattern}$$

In addition, any heddle could be lifted singly. Many patterns can be woven from the Rosepath threading draft, some of which are shown in Figs. 111 and 112. These are all drafted in Figs. 113 and 114 for the under side of the weaving. The upper side can easily be drafted from the experience gained when dealing with the box loom.

The writers strongly recommend all weavers to draft a few patterns before commencing the actual work on their loom. This not only helps the weaver to grasp the principles, but often prevents the tedious task of undoing a woven pattern. Moreover, it seems the only rational way of setting to work: designing an article before making it, as a builder designs before building his house.

In order to see the exact proportion of a pattern it will be necessary to draw the lines correctly on the draft, allowing the correct number of weft threads. Though the ordinary graph paper with 8 or 12 squares to the inch suffices for teaching the principles, it often gives a distorted idea of the woven pattern. In the drafts given in Figs. 113 and 114, only one row is shown for each weft thread, whilst in the woven borders shown in Figs. 111 and 112, two or sometimes more rows have often been worked. Compare draft with woven border No. 1. In this case four rows were woven for each pattern change.

The number given for each pattern draft corresponds with the number on the woven border in the photograph. It will be seen from the pattern drafts that four horizontal rows of squares represent the four heddles, and on these the threading draft is marked. This threading draft is again marked from right to left, along the bottom of the pattern draft, which simplifies the blocking in of the various warp threads in accordance with the heddle to be used. On the right of the pattern draft the heddles used for each particular pattern row are indicated.

118

FIG. III.—SAMPLER SHOWING BORDER DESIGNS WOVEN FROM
'ROSEPATH' THREADING DRAFT.

119

FIG. 112.—SAMPLER SHOWING BORDER DESIGNS WOVEN FROM
'ROSEPATH' THREADING DRAFT.

120

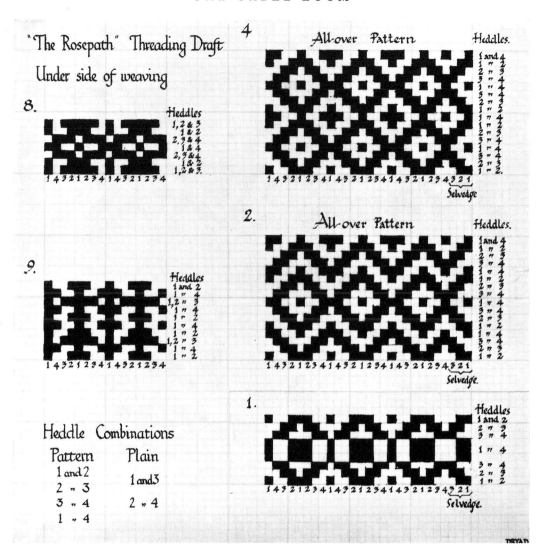

FIG. 113.

If the weaver decides to use Nos. 1 and 2 heddles, all threads on these two frames will be lifted. These can be checked with the threading draft at the foot of the pattern.

If the weaver drafts this set of patterns for herself, and then weaves them, comparing the two whilst the work is in progress, she should have no further difficulty in either reading or drafting a pattern.

Any of the threading drafts given in the next chapter can be used for the table loom.

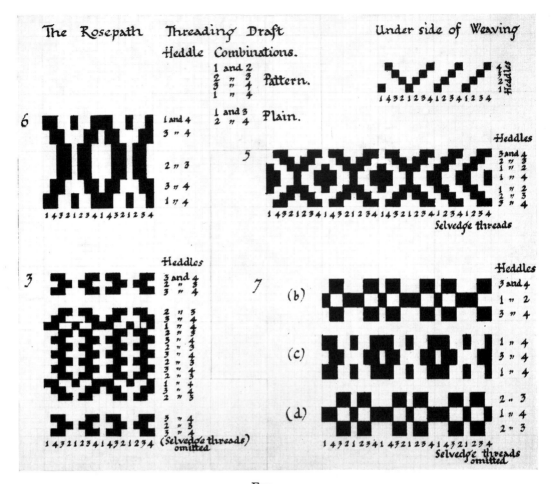

FIG. 114.

Fig. 115 shows a variety of borders woven from the Monk's Belt threading draft, and Fig. 116 several other pattern drafts, from the same order of entering.

A new threading draft will now be given, though any of those dealt with in connection with the box and table looms would be quite suitable.

The Honeysuckle threading draft, 26 threads (see Figs. 117 *a-d*), gives scope for an almost unlimited variety of patterns, some of which are drafted. The selvedge threads, 4, 3, 2, 1, 4, 3, 2, 1 (reading from the right), will be entered first—one through each heddle, and two through each dent of the reed. The twenty-six pattern threads will next be entered—one through each heddle and one through each dent until the second selvedge is reached. As the last pattern thread is entered in heddle No. 2 the first selvedge thread must be entered in

FIG. 115.—SAMPLER SHOWING BORDER DESIGNS WOVEN FROM
'MONK'S BELT' THREADING DRAFT.

heddle No. 1, the second through No. 2, third through No. 3, fourth through heddle No. 4. For this warp a 2-ply wool will be used in two shades of fawn (light and dark). These two strands will be tied together and warped in the same way as described for two strands of the same colour. On referring to the first Honeysuckle pattern draft (Fig. 117a), it will be seen that although two complete pattern repeats have been drafted, the resulting pattern does not balance. This lack of balance is less apparent in a wide piece of material with an all-over pattern; but in the case of a narrow piece of material, e.g. a scarf or a runner, it gives a more pleasing result if the pattern is balanced. On refer-ring to the pattern draft it is easily discovered that by threading a complete

123

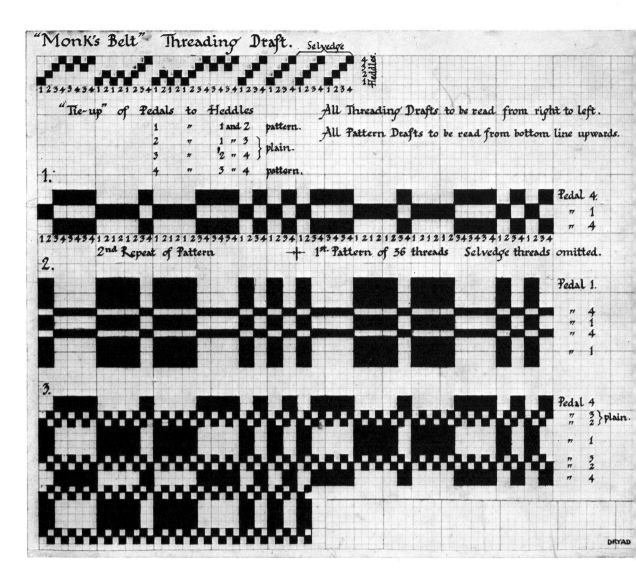

FIG. 116.

pattern of twenty-six threads and an additional seven threads, both edges of
the material will be alike. (If there are several pattern repeats, seven threads
should only be added to the last one.) A pleasing pattern can be achieved by
threading from the tenth to the twenty-fourth thread (inclusive) or from the
eighteenth to the end of the draft, and an additional sixteen threads starting
from the beginning of the draft (twenty-five threads in all).

A line drawn through the various pattern drafts will quickly make it apparent
how many threads must be entered to make a balanced pattern, and at which

124

point in the threading draft entering should be commenced and ended, to give the most pleasing results.

It will be found that, after completing the threading draft with the additional threads required for a balanced pattern, and reading from each end of the draft towards the centre, the threads will be arranged in similar groups on either side of the central thread—which in this case is on heddle 3. The Honeysuckle draft with the seven additional threads reads as follows:

141414/1212/323412/3/214323/2121/414141.

When adding additional threads to make a balanced pattern a weaver must be careful when the second selvedge is reached to enter the threads through the heddles which will fit in with the last pattern thread, as mentioned earlier in the chapter. The actual order of entering the selvedges makes no material difference to the weaving provided that the threads fit in with the last pattern thread.

Other threading drafts can be checked in the same way.

A copper-beech colour will be chosen for the weft thread. The alternate strands in light and dark fawn in the warp will facilitate the checking of the threading up; as when pedal 3 is depressed, all threads of one shade should be down—the others up. If the fabric is to be of a width necessitating eleven repeats of the pattern, then $11 \times 26 = 286$ threads will be needed. To these must be added an extra sixteen threads for the two selvedges. (Three or four double threads are usually allowed for each selvedge, but the number can be varied to suit any particular type of material.)

The warp is threaded in the usual way through heddles and reed, and the threads attached to the front roller in readiness for the weaving. The Honey-suckle Pattern Drafts on Figs. 117 *a-d* can be used for either a table or a foot-power loom. On the right-hand side of the drafts the pedals to be used are indicated, but if a weaver wants to use the drafts for a table loom she must refer to the tie-up given with the drafts; e.g. in Draft No. 1 the first pattern row is produced by pedal 1. For a table loom the same pattern is produced by using heddles 2 and 3 as these two heddles are tied to pedal 1.

In the table loom in which the heddles are pulled down the result will be the same as in a foot-power loom; but in a table loom in which the heddles are raised, the pattern as drafted for the foot-power loom will appear on the under side of the work.

Various types of Twills (see Fig. 140) can be woven on a Table Loom. Draft No. 1 on Fig. 141 indicates the usual method of threading for twills, whilst Nos. 2 and 3 show variations of the original draft.

Several patterns are drafted from each threading draft, but many others can be worked out by a weaver interested in the great variety of twills.

CHAPTER XI

The Foot-Power Loom

(COMMONLY KNOWN AS THE HAND LOOM)

IN the four-heddle box loom and the table loom previously described the weaver, in order to produce patterns, has often had to raise or lower two heddles simultaneously. In the so-called hand loom (which the reader may be tempted to say would be more accurately called a 'foot loom') time and labour are saved by the device of connecting the heddles with pedals which are operated by the feet; thus leaving the hands entirely free for the purpose of passing the shuttle through the shed.

There are many types of hand looms (some of which are illustrated), but probably the most interesting are the few well-worn old English models, relics of the early weavers, still to be found in different parts of the country. Unfortunately, these are becoming rare, as the factory system brought about the decline in home crafts, and many of the large old looms, after being relegated to a cellar or an attic, were lost or partially destroyed.

In the recent revival of crafts, many of these looms have been discovered, and brought into action. Their solidarity and age cannot help but appeal to anyone interested in the craft, as they are a definite link with the past, and have played their part in the history of inventions and occupations. Unfortunately, most of them are very large, and thus difficult for a weaver to house, unless plenty of space is available. There are, however, a vast number of smaller looms with two, four, or six pedals, on the market. Fig. 83 shows a primitive arrangement of pedals in a two-heddle loom, one pedal being attached to each heddle.

The four-pedal loom must now be considered. From working on the table loom it was discovered that heddles Nos. 1 and 3, and 2 and 4, if lifted or lowered together, lifted or lowered the alternate sets of threads.

In the foot-power loom, as each pedal is pressed the corresponding heddles are pulled down—the others being raised a similar amount (due to the working of the cords on the pulley), thus giving a better shed. This lowering of heddles will be referred to throughout the chapter.

Heddles Nos. 1 and 3 must therefore be tied to one pedal; 2 and 4 to another; 1 and 2 to a third; 3 and 4 to a fourth. Since two pedals will be required for the plain weaving, the others will be for the pattern. It is advisable to keep the two inner pedals for the plain weaving, and the two outer ones for the pattern weaving. The changes of patterns, brought about by using the pedals in a

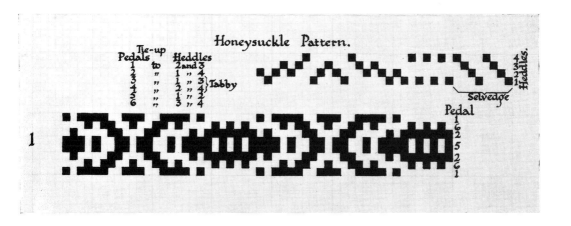

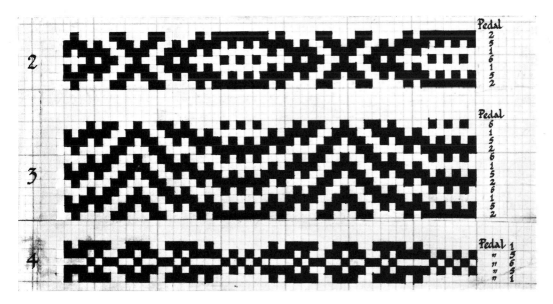

FIG. 117a.

certain order, will be obvious to the weaver. A six-pedal loom will give still greater scope for patterns, since the following pairs of heddles may be tied to any one pedal: Heddles Nos. 1 and 4, 2 and 3, 1 and 3, 2 and 4, 1 and 2, and 3 and 4. It will be seen from this that though the same threading draft may be used on the four- or six-pedal loom, the latter gives two additional interchanges of pattern. Before going further the writers will describe a Danish-type loom, as illustrated in Figs. 119a and 119b, and follow this description by working instructions for the putting on of the warp, tying of pedals to heddles, etc.

Nos. 1 and 2. The two largest parts of the loom, namely, the sides or uprights to which most parts of the loom are fitted.

FIG. 117*b*.

No. 3. The bar connecting the bottom of the two sides at the back of the loom, and fitted with two brackets supporting an iron rod on which the six treadles are slotted. Each treadle has eight holes down the centre.

No. 4. The bar connecting the bottom of the sides at the front of the loom.

No. 5. The cloth beam on which the material is wound as it is woven. It is fitted at one end with an iron cog wheel and a wooden wheel with handles which enable it to be moved round. It also has a length of calico.

No. 6. The top cross bar of the loom, to which two pulleys are fixed. The heddle horses, No. 14, are suspended from these.

No. 7. The breast beam. The weaving is taken over this to bar No. 8 and on to the cloth beam, No. 5.

No. 8. The bar immediately above the cloth beam. The weaving is taken over this bar and on to the cloth beam.

128

Honeysuckle Pattern

FIG. 117c.

No. 9. The lams, of which there are four, are similar in appearance to the treadles, with holes down the centre, but are narrower.

No. 10. The slat inserted in front of the breast beam No. 7 to protect weaving from any rubbing.

No. 11. The back frame holding the warp beam. It is fitted with a wooden cog wheel at one end and provided with a length of calico.

No. 12. The handle used for releasing the warp beam when required. It is screwed to the right-hand side upright, and connected with string to the metal piece resting on the wheel of the warp beam.

No. 13. The batten or beater. This is for holding the reed which is used for beating together the rows of weaving.

129

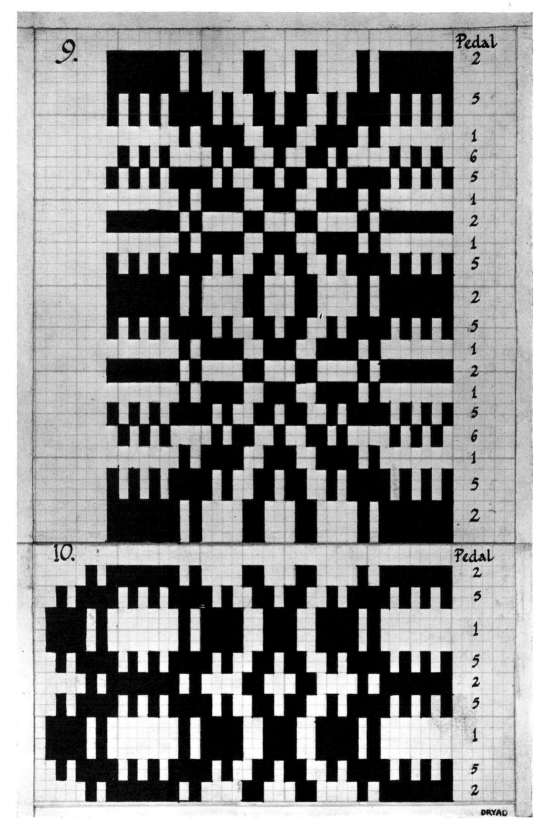

9.

Pedal
2
5
1
6
5
1
2
1
5
2
5
1
2
1
5
6
1
5
2

10.

Pedal
2
5
1
5
2
5
1
5
2

DRYAD

FIG. 117d.

8

1

4

5

7

3

2

6

DRYAD

FIG. 118.—SAMPLER SHOWING BORDERS WOVEN FROM THE 'HONEYSUCKLE THREADING DRAFT.

K

131

FIG. 119a.—Dryad Danish-type Loom, front view. FIG. 119b.—Dryad Danish-type Loom, back view.

No. 14. The heddle horses. The heddle frames are suspended from these with string.

No. 15. The heddle frame on which string heddles are mounted. String heddles are also known as healds, headles and yelds.

No. 16. The two shed sticks; these are bevelled and have a hole at either end.

No. 17. The warp sticks, of which there are twenty-four, these being inserted between the layers of warp threads in winding them on the warp beam.

Some looms are supplied with two 'castles' or comb-like turreted appliances, Fig. 120, for supporting and separating the heddles during the threading of the warp and while checking the tie-up of the loom.

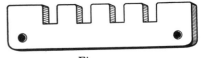

Fig. 120.

The castles are suspended from the top bar of the loom with pieces of string. Each of the heddle frames is inserted in a slot in the castle, and by this means the threading of the warp and the tying-up of the loom are greatly simplified.

Some variations from the model described are found in:

1. *The Elex Loom* (Fig. 121). This differs from the previous type in having four pulleys to replace heddle horses for slinging the heddles; in having the warp beam in a fixed position instead of movable; and in having the pedals attached to the front bar of the loom instead of to the back one.

2. *Foot Power Looms with Countermarch action* (as follows).

132

FIG. 121.—The Dryad 'Elex' Loom.

Folding Loom (Fig. 122), 34 in. reed. This is a most useful loom for a weaver who has limited space as the weaving need not be removed from the loom before folding and it can easily be carried from room to room or transported for demonstration purposes.

Jaclex Loom (Fig. 123), 30 in. reed. This is a heavy compact loom with four heddles and six pedals. It will take a warp of approximately nine yards. The countermarch action is obtained with a double set of lams which, when the pedals are depressed, allow one part of the warp to rise and the remainder to fall, thus ensuring a perfect shed, and minimising the strain on the warp.

The tying up of this type of loom appears much more complicated but should present no difficulty to a weaver who carries out the following instructions:

1. Tie the jacks together at the centre with a thin piece of cord approximately 30 in. in length.

2. From the outside hole in each jack take a cord 27 in. long to the hole at the end of each heddle bar or frame. The heddle frames will now be suspended by this cord from the jacks.

3. Take a long cord approximately 68 in. long from the centre of the cord which joins the jacks together, to meet the cord (18 in. long) from the centre hole in each of the bottom set of lams.

4. From the bottom heddle bars take a cord 14 in. long and join with a snitch knot to the one (12 in. long) from the centre hole in each of the top set of lams.

5. Now tie the top set of lams with cords approximately 28 in. long to meet

133

FIG. 122.—Dryad Folding Loom.

the pedals with cords 18 in. long, in accordance with the pattern to be
used, e.g.:

Lams 1 and 2 to pedal No. 1
,, 2 ,, 3 ,, ,, 2
,, 1 ,, 3 ,, ,, 3
,, 2 ,, 4 ,, ,, 4
,, 3 ,, 4 ,, ,, 5
,, 1 ,, 4 ,, ,, 6

(While this is being done, the bottom set of lams should be entirely
ignored.)

6. Now examine the top set of lams and note carefully any holes left vacant.
These vacant holes should be filled in the bottom set of lams, e.g. if, in
the top set of lams 1 and 4 are filled, then 2 and 3 should be filled in the
bottom set of lams, and the lams then tied to the pedals in the usual way.

If heddles 1, 2 and 3 are tied to the top set of lams then 4 should be tied to
the bottom set or vice versa. (The countermarch action is of particular advantage in cases where three heddles are lowered at the same time.)

It will be seen that there are as many ties to each pedal as there are heddle
frames—in this case—four.

Length of cord from bottom set of lams to pedals, 14 in.

Length of cord from pedals to meet this, 14 in.

3. *The Cottage Loom* (Fig. 124), is the table loom previously illustrated but
with the addition of foot-power equipment, which enables a weaver to switch
over from hand power to foot power with a minimum of expense.

134

FIG. 123.—An Overslung Batten Loom.

Again referring to the Danish loom, Fig. 119, the method of transferring the warp to the loom has already been described, also the entering of the warp threads through the heddles and reed and attaching these to the front roller. Before winding the warp (to which an extra 27 inches should be added for tying on and wastage) on to the warp beam it will be necessary, however, to remove the heddle frames, and so leave an open space through which the warp can pass.

As these are not yet tied to the lams or pedals, the heddle frames can be lifted bodily and rested on the cross beam of the loom. They can be tied in

135

position until the warp has been wound on to the warp beam, and the frames can then be lowered into position in readiness for the threading up.

It will be seen from Fig. 125 that the heddles are in this case tied to heddle horses—these in turn being attached to either end of a string running over a pulley —the string being sufficiently long to give free movement up or down to the heddles and allow for tying.

Another string loop suspended from each end of the heddle horses supports the heddle frames (Fig. 125). These loops should be of such a length that the eyes of the heddles are in line horizontally with the centre of the reed.

The earlier looms had no lams, which meant that the heddles were tied directly to the pedals. The provision of lams simplified

FIG. 124.—Dryad Cottage Loom with foot-power adaptation.

the tying up, and enabled the weaver to get a direct pull from the centre of the heddle, resulting in a better shed. Each of the lams has a hole in line with the centre of the heddle frame, and a string is passed through this hole and attached to a special non-slip loop suspended from each heddle (Fig. 126). The string loop used for attaching the heddle frames to the heddle horses, and again to the lams (see Fig. 127), is easy to manipulate, and by it the height of the heddle frames can be regulated. In addition, each lam has a series of holes in line with the pedals, and through these the strings can pass and tie to the loop, which passes through a hole in the pedal (in the same way as shown in Fig. 127). It will be seen from this that as each lam is tied directly to each heddle, if a lam is pulled down, its corresponding heddle will be pulled down also.

Therefore, if the lams are tied to the pedals, it will give the same result as tying the heddle frames to the pedals. The lams should now be tied as follows:

Lams 2 and 3 to pedal No. 1
,,   1 ,, 4   ,,   ,,   2
,,   1 ,, 3   ,,   ,,   3

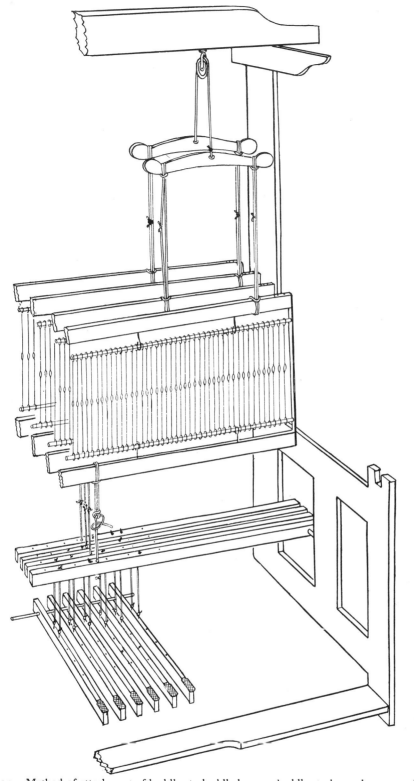

FIG. 125.—Method of attachment of heddles to heddle horses ; heddles to lams ; lams to pedals.

Lams 2 and 4 to pedal No. 4
" 1 " 2 " " 5
" 3 " 4 " " 6

To simplify this tying up and save time in readjusting the string, which frequently stretches while the weaving is being done, the writers have found an 'eye bolt' a useful addition to the loom. This is quite inexpensive, and can be procured at any ironmonger's at very little cost. This eye bolt takes the place of the

FIG. 126.—Method of making non-slip loop and knot.

string loop previously mentioned, and is passed through a hole in the pedal, with the eye on top (Fig. 128). A small wing nut is then screwed on to the bolt above the pedal and another underneath, and after the loom has been tied up and the weaving commenced, if the string is found to have stretched it can be readjusted by the nut instead of untying the knot in the string. (A knot, after being pulled very tight, is often most difficult to manipulate.) It will be seen from the sketch that each pedal has a series of holes along its length to line up vertically with the holes in the lams, which are above and at right angles to the pedals. In order to ensure that the tying up is as perfect as possible, it is best, after entering and attaching the warp threads to the front roller, to tie

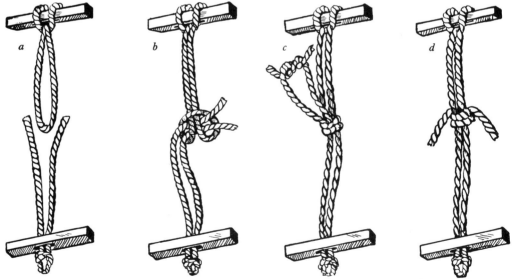

FIG. 127.—Details of non-slip knot for attaching heddles to pedals and lams.

FIG. 128.—Eye bolt

the four heddle frames together at each end or fix them in castles (as previously described) while the lams and heddles are tied, then, after attaching them to the lams with pieces of tightly twisted strong string, and seeing that the latter hang evenly (they should have a slight upward tilt), tie these together before attaching to the pedals with similar pieces of string. The pedals should also hang evenly at the same height from the floor and within easy access of the foot (the height can be tested by the weaver when sitting at the loom). If the pedals are too high from the floor, they are difficult to operate, a strain on the weaver, and sometimes interfere with the free movement of the lams. Though on the surface this tying up of the loom seems a somewhat trivial operation, it is, nevertheless, of the utmost importance. The weaver will be well advised to spare neither time nor effort in carrying out this part of the work, for a well-set-up loom is like a well-tuned engine, and will result in smooth and efficient running.

The tying up complete, the shuttle must now be prepared for weaving.

The stick shuttle, used up to this stage, may now be replaced by the more nimble boat-shaped shuttle, with a separate spindle for the bobbin.

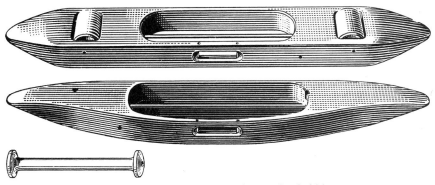

FIG. 129.—Two shuttles and a wooden bobbin.

There are two types of shuttle, with or without rollers (see Fig. 129), either of which is satisfactory. Care must be taken in winding the bobbins for the shuttles. To facilitate this, a bobbin winder (Fig. 130) is attached to a small bracket on the loom.

A small oval piece of moderately stiff paper is wound round the spindle of the bobbin winder, and the end of the wool secured in the roll. To prevent the wool from running over the edge of the bobbin it will be advisable to wind a few layers first at one end and then the other, giving two raised portions. The subsequent layers should be guided to and fro between the two raised ends, until the bobbin appears as in Fig. 131b. If the wool is allowed to run over the edge of the bobbin and become loose, it will give endless trouble when weaving. Alternatively, a small wooden bobbin, Fig. 129, could be used if preferred. This type of bobbin is especially useful when working with linen thread or similar springy yarn. The bobbin is then taken from the winder and slipped on to the wire of the shuttle. To do this, move the wire (hinged at one end) out of the L-shaped groove. Slip the bobbin on to the wire and refix it in the groove. The end of the wool is threaded through the slot in the shuttle, so that the wool will unwind from the underside of the spool. Before actually beginning to weave, the tension of the warp should be adjusted, the threads being firm and taut; and the warp should be drawn together with a few rows of weaving, as described in the previous chapters.

It will be well to do a few inches of plain weaving before beginning the pattern. Before doing this insert a shed stick in one of the sheds—then start weaving by passing a thread through the next shed. The stick will give a firm edge against which to beat the weft. If the warp threads have been tied carefully to the front shed stick before beginning to weave, it should only be necessary to weave a few rows in order to space out the threads evenly. Errors in entering the threads should be carefully checked and rectified at this stage.

FIG. 130.—
Bobbin winder.

Any scrap of thread can be used for the weft in these first few rows and as soon as the warp threads appear to be evenly spaced, the special weft thread for the particular article should be used. Wastage should be kept to a minimum. Approximately one inch of 'scrap' weaving should suffice. Still keeping the same order adopted while working on the table loom, when pedal 3 (pulling down heddles 1 and 3) is depressed the shuttle is thrown from right to left. When pedal 4 (pulling down heddles 2 and 4) is depressed the shuttle is thrown from left to right. The right foot should be used for pedal 3, the left foot for pedal 4. Thus the throwing of the shuttle with the right and left hand alternately coincides with the movement of the feet. For the plain weaving one foot only may be used, transferring this from one pedal to the other. In pattern-weaving it will undoubtedly prove more satisfactory to use both feet.

In practice it will be found that the weft thread is beaten up more tightly if the reed or batten is pulled towards the weaver while the shed is still open. For weaving in wool, this beating up should be done quite lightly and easily, as a loose texture looks more effective when off the loom. Should a warp thread break during the process of weaving, it can be mended in the following way: join a new piece of wool on to the broken end (behind the heddles) with a weaver's knot. This knot is made in the following way: take the two threads which are to be joined together, and place the left-hand over the right-hand one as shown in Fig. 132a. Then pass the long right-hand thread

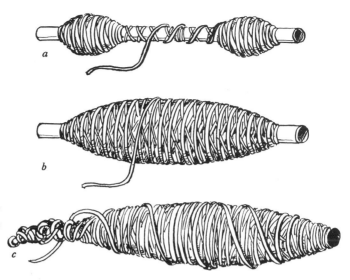

FIG. 131.—(a) Method of starting bobbin; (b) well-wound bobbin; (c) badly wound bobbin.

over the thumb, round the back of the short end pointing to the left, in front of the other short end, and let it hang down towards the right, holding the loop just made between the thumb and finger (Fig. 132b). Next pass the short end

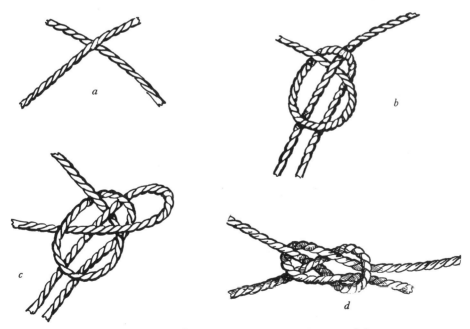

FIGS. 132a, b, c, and d.—Stages in the making of a weaver's knot

pointing towards the right down through this loop and out on the opposite side, holding this down under the thumb (Fig. 132c). Tighten the knot by pulling the long end which hangs down towards the right (Fig. 132d).

Thread the new piece through the correct heddle and dent of the reed, then wrap the loose end round a pin in the woven fabric—the pin being in line with the warp thread. The weaving can then proceed, and when complete the end of the thread can be darned into the fabric and cut off close to the work. As a few inches of weaving are done, the fabric should be wound on to the cloth beam and the warp threads off the warp beam simultaneously, and the weaving continued as before. This is done by lifting the catch from the ratchet, and turning the handle attached to the roller. The weaver should now be ready for pattern-weaving.

Several patterns have been drafted in Figs. 117a-d, and other borders have been woven on the sampler shown in Fig. 118, the numbers of which correspond with those shown on the pattern drafts. The reader should now be able to draft a series of borders, and from them choose those suitable for the runner or cushion for which the warp has been made. In order to get a more accurate idea of the border, it could be drafted and coloured on the squared paper.

If a scarf is being woven with strips of pattern-weaving at each end, the weaver must keep a record of the pattern rows used on the first end of the scarf—as this will be wound on to the roller and thus hidden from view by the time the other end of the scarf is reached.

142

FIG. 133.—CURTAINS IN COARSE KNITTING COTTON.

FIG. 134.—WOOL CURTAINS.

As the tension of the weaving varies, it is best to measure the stripes and keep these uniform rather than count the number of rows.

In addition to weaving with wool, it is possible, on the hand loom, to weave in cotton and silk.

Whatever material—whether silk, cotton, or wool—may be used for the warp, it should be composed of very evenly spun and tightly twisted strands, in order to withstand the great amount of strain imposed upon it when adjusting the tension of the warp. The weft threads need not be quite so tightly spun. (Hand-spun wool should only be used for the weft at this stage.) As a short piece of warp is wasted in the tying on at the beginning of a piece of work, it is advisable to put on a sufficient amount of warp for several articles, and weave all before taking the material from the loom.

143

If, however, for some reason, one piece of the work is needed, the weaver can avoid excessive waste in the following way: when the scarf, or particular article, is completed, a few additional inches should be woven (beating the weft up tightly), then a warp stick should be inserted in one of the sheds, and another inch of fairly tight weaving should be done. The finished scarf may then be cut off, and the warp stick, which is threaded into the fabric, should be attached to the front roller in the usual way, when the weaving may proceed. If another warp is required for the same pattern it saves considerable time in threading up a detailed pattern if the warp threads are knotted on to the old warp, a short length of which has been left on the warp beam. A new warp is made in the usual way and each thread is tied to a thread of the old warp just in front of the reed. This completed, the warp is wound on to the warp beam carefully, to avoid breaking the knots in the reed or heddles. When the end of the warp is reached, this is tied in bunches to the front roller in the usual way, before beginning to weave.

Having woven scarves, cushion squares and other small articles on the foot-power loom, a weaver may now like to attempt longer lengths of materials for dresses, curtains, etc. Fig. 133 shows a pair of curtains, suitable for a kitchen or bath room, in coarse knitting cotton in Monk's Belt pattern (8 threads to the inch). 4-ply wool can also be used (12 threads per inch) for interesting door curtains, knee rugs, etc. Fig. 134 shows three curtains woven in wool with coloured honeysuckle borders.

Net curtains can easily be woven on any 2- or 4-heddle table or foot-power loom.

Fig. 135 shows six samples of curtain material woven on the same warp. This consisted of fine unbleached cotton and knitting cotton used in the following order:

Selvedge: 8 threads of knitting cotton.
Pattern: 12 fine threads, 6 coarse, 12 fine, 2 coarse.

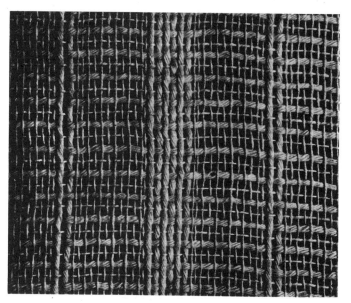

This order should be repeated to the desired width and then 8 coarse threads added for the second selvedge.

Pattern No. 1:
Weft: 1 fine thread,
1 coarse.
Repeat.

Fig. 135.

Fig. 135. (contd)

Pattern No. 2:
    Weft threads used in same order
as in the warp:
        12 fine threads.
        6 coarse ,,
        12 fine   ,,
        2 coarse ,,
        Repeat.

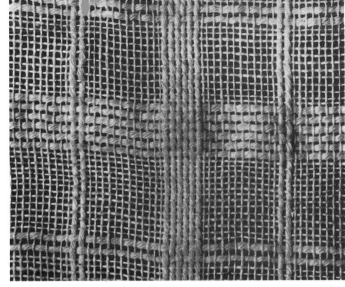

Pattern No. 3:
    Weft: 12 rows crinkle cotton.
        2 rows thick gimp.
        Repeat.

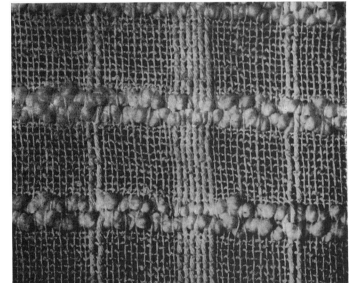

Pattern No. 4:
    Weft: 12 rows fine crinkle cotton.
        1 row thick gimp.
        6 rows crinkle.
        2 rows knitting cotton
        6 rows crinkle.
        1 row thick gimp.
        Repeat.

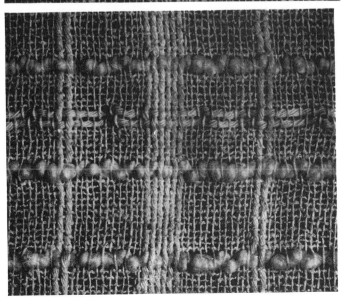

Fig. 135. (*contd.*)

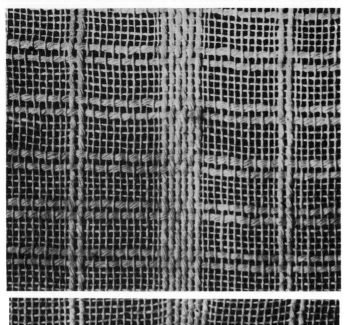

Pattern No. 5:
Weft: 4 rows fine cotton.
2 rows knitting cotton (same as used in warp).
Repeat.

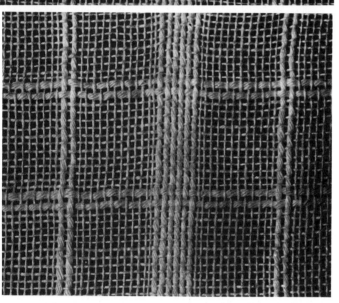

Pattern No. 6:
12 rows fine unbleached cotton.
2 rows knitting cotton (same threads as in warp).

Interesting effects can also be produced by spaced warps. Fig. 136*a* gives an indication of the type of material which can be produced in this way. The sample was woven with unbleached cotton and consists solely of tabby weave. The material wears well, drapes nicely and improves with washing.

The warp threads should be entered as follows:
40 threads (2 per dent) for plain stripe
Miss one dent
Three threads in next dent
Miss one dent
One thread in next dent
Repeat for desired width (14 dent reed)

Fig. 136a.

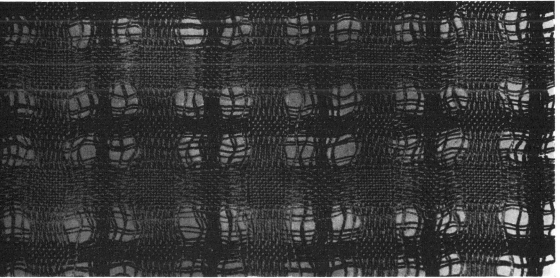

Fig. 136b.

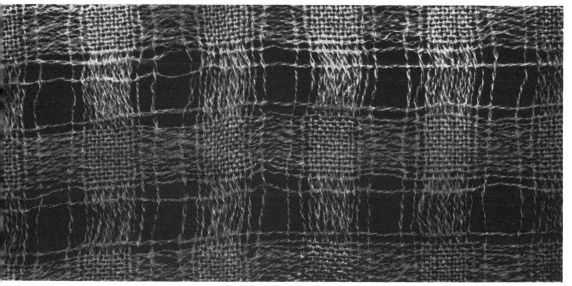

Fig. 136c.

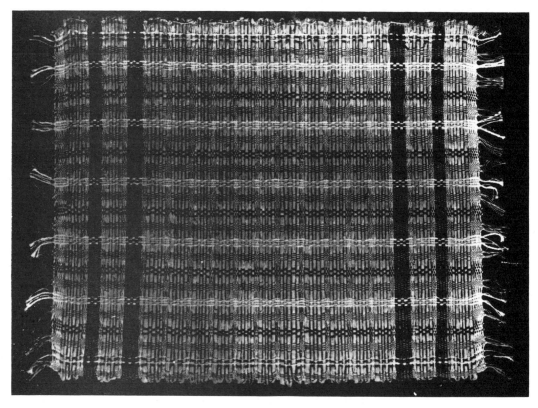

FIG. 137.—RAFFIA TABLE MAT.

Another type of net curtain can be woven as follows:
Threading Draft (reading from right to left)

$$\underbrace{3\underbrace{2}3—4—3\underbrace{2}3—4—3\underbrace{2}3}_{C}—\underbrace{4}{}\underline{4\underbrace{1}4\underbrace{1}4\underbrace{1}4\underbrace{1}}$$

C   B A

Repeat A for 2 in. or as desired (one per dent)
    ,,   B ,, $\frac{1}{2}$ in. ,,   ,,   (two   ,,   )
    ,,   C ,, 4 in. ,,   ,,
Note: ⌣ = 1 *dent*
        — = *miss* 1 *dent*
Unless indicated as above, there should be one thread per dent.
Tie up. Heddles 1 and 3   to   Pedal 1
          ,,   2 and 4   to   ,, 2
          ,,   1, 2 and 3   to   ,, 3
Pedals should be used in the following order:
    32123212321 (reading from right to left)

148

Many pleasing effects can be produced by omitting some of the dents in the reed, e.g. if there are 36 threads to the inch a reed with 18 dents to the inch is used. Nine dents could be threaded and nine left vacant, or an occasional dent or group of dents could be omitted at intervals when threading the warp. The same spaces should be allowed in the weft. A gauge, e.g. a narrow strip of wood, cardboard or cane, can be used as an aid in getting all spaces equal, but after a little experience a weaver should find this unnecessary.

Fig. 136*b* shows a piece of curtain made with this type of spaced warp in fine cotton 32 threads per inch, while Fig. 136*c* shows a similar piece woven in fine wool (the latter could also be useful for light scarves, or stoles).

As cotton curtain material is inclined to shrink when washed, the authors strongly recommend weavers to allow very generous hems when making up the curtains.

Another way in which spaced warps can be used is indicated in the raffia table mat, Fig. 137.

A warp can be made with any oddments of cotton in many thicknesses and colours (a useful way in which to use up odd bits of yarn left over from various warps).

The warp can be spaced in various ways to suit individual taste, though only two or three dents should be left empty, otherwise the work would be too loose.

The sample was woven with coloured raffia interspersed with a few rows of linen thread, giving a most pleasing effect to the finished article.

The warp could also be crossed with single strands of raffia (projecting at each selvedge to form a fringe); while strips of rush, cane, straw could also be used.

Other ideas will no doubt suggest themselves to a weaver with originality and ingenuity.

A plain reversible fabric (double weave), having one colour on one side and another on the other, can be woven on any loom having four heddles (see threading draft No. 33. Thread loom up with alternate black and white threads, 1, 2, 3, 4. Tie pedals as follows:

Heddles		Pedals
3	to	1
1 and 3 and 4	to	2
1	to	3
1 and 2 and 3	to	4

It requires two shuttles, one black and one white, for weaving. To begin, press pedal 4 and pass black thread through shed; then pedal 3 and pass white thread through; pedal 2 and pass black thread through; pedal 1 and pass white thread through. Repeat in this order. This will give a black cloth on upper side

Fig. 138.

and white on the under side. The warp threads for this type of weaving should be spaced twice as close as for plain tabby weave as half the warp threads are on the upper, and half on the lower side of the work, and there must be an odd number of threads in the warp.

Bags without seams at the bottom can be woven with two rows of weft on the under side of the weaving, alternating with two on the upper side—the fabric being joined at one selvedge only to form the bottom of the bag.

In a similar way a circular or tubular bag as shown in Fig. 138 can be woven, but in this case only one row of weft on the upper alternates with one on the under side, the weaving being joined at both selvedges.

An extra piece of fabric was woven to cover the stiffened base and a braid woven for the handle which was stitched down both sides of the bag to give added strength. A hand-made cord and covered brass rings provided a suitable finish to an attractive piece of work.

The warp for the bag consisted of cream cotton (twenty threads to the inch). Various types and thicknesses of cotton were used for the weft, e.g. green, red, yellow and blue knitting cotton; fine black cotton, crinkle and loop cotton, etc.

A bag of this type offers great scope to the weaver for the introduction of different types and colours of yarn to give interesting texture and colour effects.

CHAPTER XII

Tweeds

TWEEDS can be successfully woven on table or foot-power looms. Good Cheviot or Harris Tweed yarn can be bought in varying thicknesses or 'cuts' and is suitable for weaving from 12 to 24 threads to the inch. Details of yarn are given in the chapter 'Materials for Use'.

The yarn is generally woven in the grease. As difficulty is sometimes experienced with the selvedge threads in weaving tweeds, it is advisable to use a more tightly spun two or three-ply wool for the selvedge threads. As an alternative, weavers can use two-ply botany wool for warp with tweed yarn for weft.

A great variety of patterns can be woven from the simple threading draft 1, 2, 3, 4, by altering the sequence of the order in which the pedals are used and varying the tie-up of the heddles to the pedals, etc.

The writers strongly recommend all weavers to experiment in weaving as many variations as possible from this simplest of all drafts, and in so doing, realise the tremendous scope it offers for both colour and texture effect, and become more familiar with the functions of the loom.

If heddles 1 and 3 are tied to one pedal and 2 and 4 to another and the pedals used alternately a plain tabby weave will result: whilst a hopsack can be produced by threading two threads through adjacent heddles, viz. 11, 22, 33, 44, and using the pedals in the same way. Two rows of weft should be inserted in each shed.

This can best be done by using two shuttles and passing each in turn through the shed. This avoids any twisting of the weft threads.

The patterns most generally used for tweeds are:
1. Twill.
2. Reversed or broken twill.
3. Herringbone.
4. Bird eye twill.
5. Goose eye.
6. Wheat ear. This gives a similar result to the herringbone but with a narrower stripe.
7. Rosepath.
8. Diamond.
9. Many of the other small patterns used for linen weaves.

Twill should be threaded 1, 2, 3, 4. Repeat.

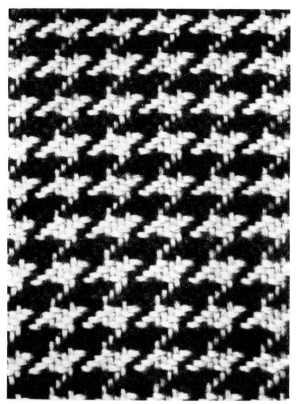

FIG. 139.—A POPULAR TWILL WEAVE
(REVERSIBLE BROKEN CHECK).

The tie-up is as follows:

Heddles	Pedals
1 and 2	1
2 and 3	2
3 and 4	3
1 and 4	4

The pedals can be used in sequence either way, giving a left or right-hand twill.

One of the most popular twill patterns for tweed—a reversible broken check (Fig. 139) can be produced as follows:

Thread four black threads and four white threads alternately, in the order 4, 3, 2, 1 (reading from right to left). The loom should be tied up as indicated for twill patterns, and the weft should be inserted with four rows of black alternated with four rows of white yarn. By altering the tie-up of the pedals, other interesting weaves can be accomplished. It would be advisable for a beginner to draft these on squared paper.

Another popular pattern for tweeds is threaded as follows:

2, 3, 4, 3, 2, 1. Repeat.

For this the loom should be tied as indicated:

Heddles		Pedals
1 and 2	to	1
2 and 4	to	2
3 and 4	to	3
1 and 4	to	4

The pedals should be used in the order 1, 2, 3, 4.

From drafting this on squared paper the weaver will see that one pattern row (over 3, under 3) is followed by a tabby row.

The second pattern row (under 3, over 3) is followed by the alternate tabby row.

The result, particularly when a different colour is used for warp and weft, is most pleasing.

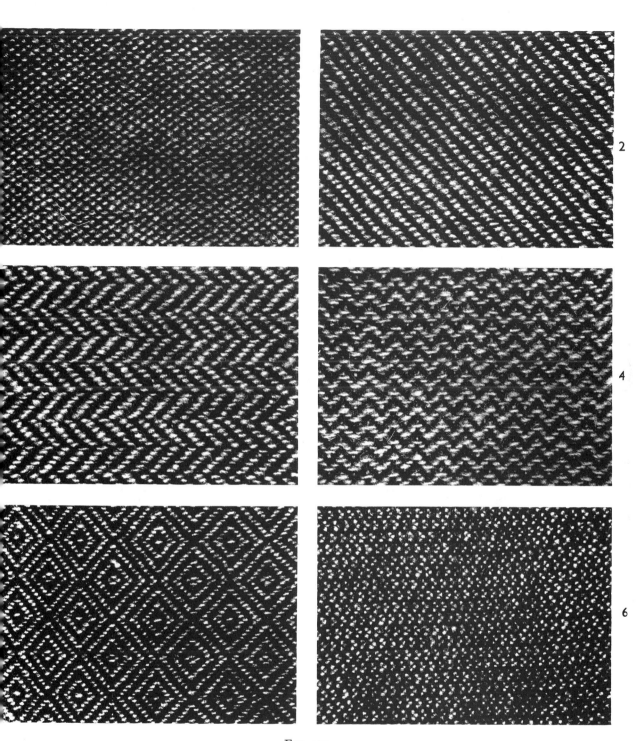

FIG. 140.

1. PLAIN WEAVE.
3. REVERSE TWILL.
5. GOOSE EYE.

2. TWILL.
4. HERRINGBONE.
6. BIRD EYE.

153

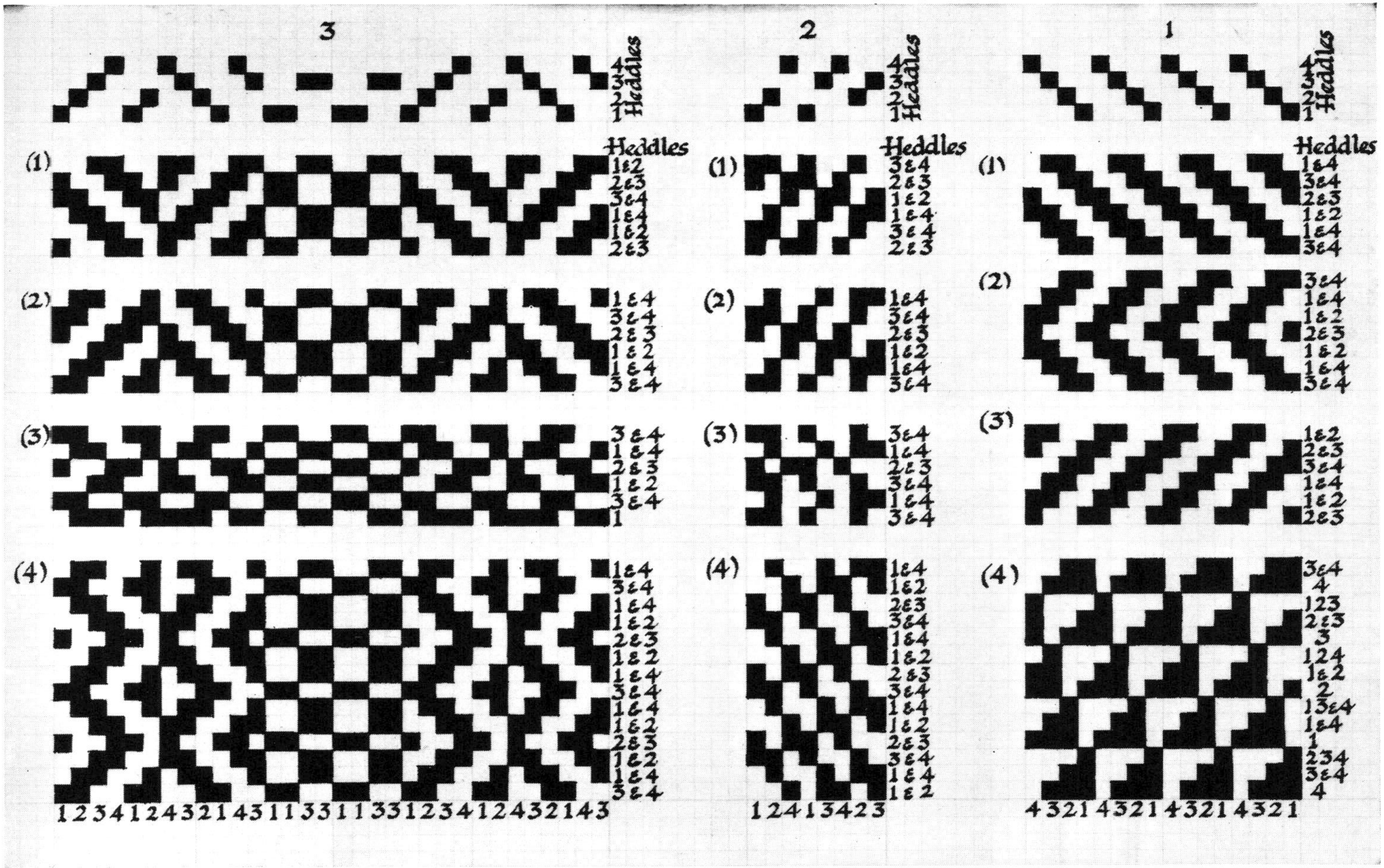

FIG. 141.—PATTERN DRAFTS FOR TWILLS. (*To be used in conjunction with the written instructions.*)

In addition, some of the above patterns can be combined quite successfully to lend added interest, e.g.

> Hopsack and Tabby.
> Hopsack and Twill
> Tabby and Twill.

The width of the stripes of each type of weave can be varied to suit individual taste.

Fig. 142 shows an example of the combination of Tabby and Twill.

The material was woven with Harris tweed weft in brown, beige and yellow on a fine two-ply botany warp in beige.

All six pedals were used and tied up as follows:

Heddles		Pedals	
1 and 2	to	1	
2 and 3	to	2	
3 and 4	to	3	Twill
1 and 4	to	4	
1 and 3	to	5	
2 and 4	to	6	Tabby

Four rows of plain tabby alternated with four rows of twill weaving. One twill stripe was woven in brown: the alternate stripe with one brown, two yellow and one brown row.

The twill stripes give a raised and interesting effect to the fabric.

Fig. 141 shows some variations of the usual twill threading and several drafted patterns from each.

Interesting effects can be achieved by introducing stripes of different colours in the weft or in both warp and weft, e.g.

1. 3 brown, 3 beige alternately in warp—beige weft.
2. 3 brown, 3 beige alternately in warp and weft.
3. Beige warp—3 beige, 3 brown alternately in weft.
4. 4 dark, 4 light alternately in warp and weft (groups reversed at intervals).
5. 3 dark, 3 medium, 3 light in warp and weft.
6. 2 dark, 1 light in warp and weft.
7. 3 dark, 2 medium, 1 light in warp and weft.
8. 2 dark, 2 light warp: 1 dark, 1 light weft.
9. 4 dark, 4 light warp: 2 dark, 2 light weft.

In weaving twills it is sometimes found that the end thread of the selvedges is not caught by each throw of the weft.

If the threads of the warp are entered in the order 1, 2, 3, 4, and the pedals used in the same order, the weaving should be so arranged that when using pedal 1 and pedal 3 the weft passes from left to right, and from right to left when using the other two pedals.

When the order of using the pedals, however, does not correspond with the order of entering the warp, e.g. reversed twills, etc., difficulty with the selvedges often arises. This can be overcome by breaking the weft thread and passing two rows of weft from the same side of the warp (though not, of course, through the same shed) and continuing the weaving as before.

An alternative method is to have the last selvedge thread at each edge 'floating', i.e. threaded through the dent of the reed but not

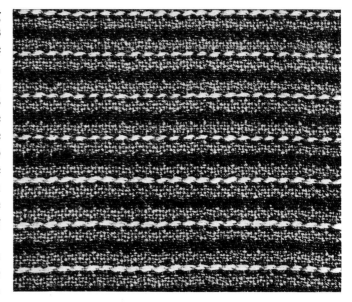

Fig. 142.

through the heddle. A weaver will find it quite easy to pass the shuttle over or under this thread as required.

By using squared paper, a weaver will quickly realise that if the selvedge thread is caught in each time, the direction in which each weft thread passes must correspond to certain sheds.

The *scouring and finishing* of tweeds is a very specialised business and the writers strongly recommend weavers to have their long lengths of tweed treated by the professional. The cost per yard for this service is quite moderate and this fact, coupled with the really 'finished' look of the material more than justifies the expense.

Small lengths of tweed can however be treated quite successfully at home by weavers who have time at their disposal and will carry out the following suggestions.

Scouring consists of washing the material thoroughly in several lots of hot water to which a generous supply of good quality soap flakes has been added. To assist in removing the grease a small quantity of ammonia can be added to the water.

The secrets of good scouring and finishing are:
1. To use plenty of hot water in a large vessel.
2. To keep the water at an even temperature as far as possible.
3. To keep the cloth moving in the water to assist in the cleansing and shrinking.

156

4. To pound the cloth with the hands (or feet) or rub on a board to assist in the shrinking process.

5. To rinse thoroughly in several lots of water of the same temperature until all trace of soap has been removed.

After scouring, all surplus water should be squeezed from the cloth and it should then be hung on rollers to dry for at least twenty-four hours, changing the position of the cloth on the rollers from time to time to avoid marks on the material.

When nearly dry the material should be covered with a damp cloth and then pressed with a moderately hot iron. The iron should be moved frequently over the surface to avoid leaving any imprint, but should be moved gently to eliminate any stretching of the material.

After pressing, the material should be tapped gently all over with a flat piece of wood or the back of a brush (a method used by tailors) to release all steam. Then the material should be hung loosely over rollers till thoroughly dry and then rolled on a cardboard or wooden foundation to avoid unnecessary creases.

CHAPTER XIII

Pattern Drafting

IN this chapter is given a series of threading drafts which will be useful to the hand-loom weaver. These drafts should be used in conjunction with the written instructions given for each. There are several really good books on this subject (details given in the Bibliography), but many are either too expensive or the drafts too elaborate for the work confined to a loom with four heddles and six pedals, though many of these drafts may be adapted by omitting some of the repeats in the pattern. Usually the threading draft acts as the treadling draft also, and is read in the following way:

'Honeysuckle' Threading Draft

21/2323/41/23/21/43/23/2121/414141

Reading from the right it will be seen that the first combination of threads used is 1 and 4; therefore, the pedal pulling down heddles 1 and 4 must be pressed down as many times as there are threads in that section of the pattern: in this case six, with, of course, a binder after each pattern row. The next combination in the threading draft is 1, 2; therefore, the pedal pulling down those heddles must be used four times.

The next change is 3, 2, and as this is only given once, two rows must be woven. Continuing the reading of the draft the weaver will discover that two rows must next be woven on pedal pulling down 3 and 4; two on heddles 1 and 2; two on 2 and 3; two on 1 and 4; four on 2 and 3; two on 1 and 2. The weaver will realise that the width of material covered by any particular pattern combination is determined by the number of threads used in that particular section of threading draft. This cannot be altered after the entering has been completed, but since the length of the pattern is controlled by the number of throws of the weft, this is in the hands of the weaver, and can be changed at will. Therefore, though the threading draft may show eight rows in any one combination, these can be lessened or increased if preferred.

When other patterns are drafted by the weaver, the special treadling draft must be indicated by numbers written at the side of each pattern row (see Fig. 117a). For reference, the weaver should include with the draft details of reed and type of warp used. This record can be amplified by samples of material woven from this draft, together with details of the dye used for producing the colours in the particular fabric. It should be borne in mind that as the design is often much more broken up on the under side than on the upper or right side of the fabric, it may be much more pleasing: both sides of the

1. Check Threading Draft.

FIG. 143.

weaving can, however, be used effectively in making up cushions, dresses, etc. Other drafts and illustrations will now be given.

1. *Check Threading Draft.* This gives a small check pattern 3 threads up and 3 down, and is most useful and effective for scarves. For this the heddles should be tied as follows:

Heddles				Pedals
1 and 2	–	–	–	1
1 and 3	Tabby	–	–	2
2 and 4	,,	–	–	3
3 and 4	–	–	–	4

It must be remembered that the pedals are numbered from right to left, and that the entering begins from the right of the threading draft. The border in Fig. 143 was woven in red and black stripes on a white scarf and produced a most pleasing effect for such a simple threading draft.

159

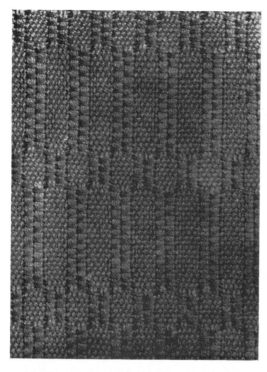

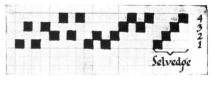

2. Ms and Os.

FIG. 144.—THREE VARIATIONS OF
MS AND OS.

160

2. A traditional pattern draft known as Ms and Os, with sixteen threads, can be utilised for a four-pedal loom, but in this case, as in all linen weaves, no binder is used. By tying heddles 2 and 4 to the first; 1 and 3 to the second; 3 and 4 to the third, and 1 and 2 to the fourth pedal an effective pattern can be produced by using pedals in the following order:

$$
\left.\begin{array}{ll}
\text{1 then 2} & \text{4 times} \\
\text{3 then 4} & \text{4 times}
\end{array}\right\}\text{twice}
$$

1 then 2   4 times

3 then 4   12 times

Other variations can be produced by altering the order in which the pedals are used.

Other patterns can be drafted by the worker.

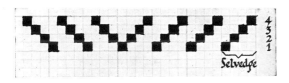

3. Goose Eye.

3. *Goose Eye* (22 threads).—The last thread shown in the draft is the first thread of the next pattern. This gives an all-over diamond pattern similar to the Rosepath border No. 2 shown in Fig. 113. A herringbone pattern can be produced from this threading draft by using the pedals in the order 4, 3, 2, 1, repeat; and a diamond pattern by using them in the order 2, 3, 4, 1, 2, 3, 4, 1, 2, 3, 4, 3, 2, 1, 4, 3, 2, 1, 4, 3, 2, 1; repeat.
This is a most suitable pattern for material in linen or wool. Tie-up as follows:

(1)

Heddles				Pedals
1 and 2	–	–	–	1
2 and 3	–	–	–	2
3 and 4	–	–	–	3
1 and 4	–	–	–	4

Herringbone and Goose Eye Patterns are excellent for a close fine weave for simple effects, and can be varied in a number of ways.

The warp should be somewhat closer than for plain tabby weave and the weft should be more firmly beaten up. Only one shuttle is used for the weaving and no binder is required.

For heavier materials a binder can be used which would need two extra pedals, one tied to heddles 1 and 3; the other to 2 and 4.

Fig. 145a shows a woollen front woven from this draft.

161

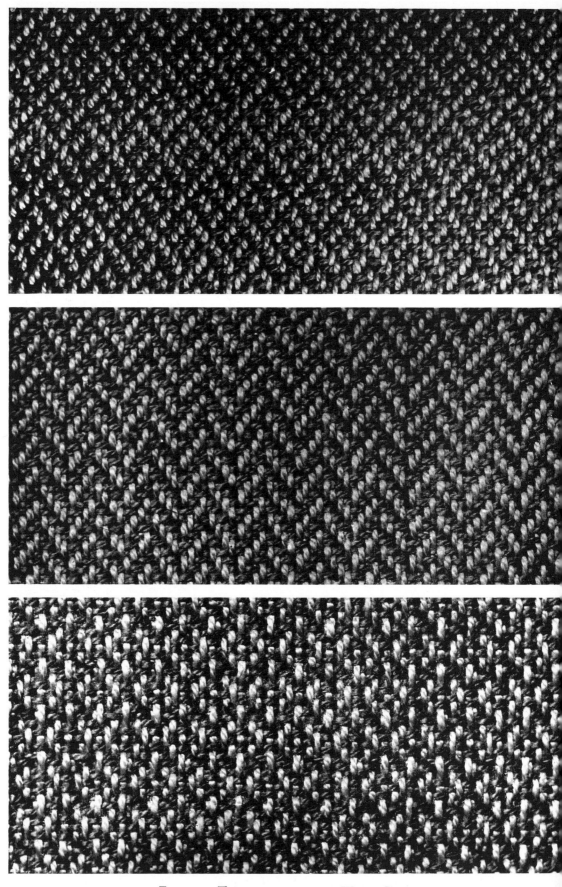

FIG. 145.—THREE VARIATIONS OF WHEAT EAR.

FIG. 145a.—FRONTS AND GAUNTLETS WOVEN BY CHILDREN AGED 12

3a. Goose Eye Adaptation.

3a. *Goose Eye Adaptation* (58 threads).—A most useful pattern for linen towels and luncheon cloths; wool or linen dress materials, etc. The tie-up is the same as for Goose Eye No. 3.

4. Wheat Ear.

4. *Wheat Ear.* This is a most useful pattern for linen, tweeds and upholstery. It requires no binder (in common with many of the other linen weaves) and has only eight threads to a pattern.

The loom should be tied in the same way as for Twills, viz.

Heddles		Pedals
1 and 2	to	1
2 and 3	to	2
3 and 4	to	3
1 and 4	to	4

Pedals should be used in the following order: 1, 4, 3, 2, then repeat.
Another pattern can be produced by using pedals 1, 4, 1, 2, repeat.
Other variations can be worked out by the weaver.

M

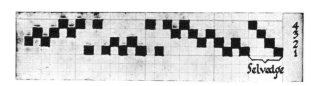

5. Russian Diaper.

FIG. 146.

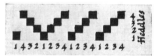

6. Rosepath.

FIG. 146a.

164

5. *Russian Diaper.*—This has a total of 26 threads to each pattern, and is very suitable for small work, and it can also be used quite successfully as a border to some of the other patterns, for curtains, covers, etc. It can be used for linen, wool or cotton. Three extra threads are required for a balanced pattern. The border shown, Fig. 146, was woven from this draft on a table loom, using the heddles in the following order:

4 rows raising heddles 1 and 2
4 ,, ,, ,, 1 ,, 4
4 ,, ,, ,, 3 ,, 4
6 ,, ,, ,, 2 ,, 3
4 ,, ,, ,, 3 ,, 4
4 ,, ,, ,, 1 ,, 4
4 ,, ,, ,, 1 ,, 2

The narrower border was produced in the same way, but only two rows instead of four were woven, using each set of heddles. Two complete repeats of the pattern were woven. In this border the coloured thread was used for the background only.

6. *Rosepath* (8 threads)—the first eight threads on the draft being used for selvedge.

This is one of the most popular drafts and is most suitable for beginners to use for their early experiments. It offers great scope for variety in both colour and pattern.

The sampler illustrated on pages 119 and 120 shows a variety of woven patterns and the illustrations in Fig. 146*a* were woven as borders in black and red on a white background, for small aprons.

Selvedge

36 threads

7. Monk's Be

FIG. 147.

7. *Monk's Belt.*—This has been dealt with fully in Chapter X.

Fig. 147 shows a scarf with a variety of borders woven from this threading draft.

8. Tortoise

FIG. 148.

8. *Tortoise* (40 threads, exclusive of selvedge).—The mat illustrated was woven in accordance with this threading draft.

166

FIG 149.

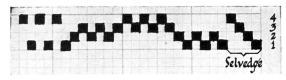

9. Turkey Foot.

9. *Turkey Foot* (24 threads).—The mat shown above was woven on a table loom from this draft. The first border was produced as follows:

6 rows raising heddles 1 and 4
6 „   „   „ 2 „ 3
6 „   „   „ 3 „ 4
6 „   „   „ 1 „ 2
6 „   „   „ 3 „ 4
6 „   „   „ 2 „ 3
6 „   „   „ 1 „ 4

The second border was produced by weaving two rows on each of the two following heddle combinations, 1 and 4; 3 and 4. The third border was produced in the same way as No. 1, but with only two rows of weaving on each heddle combination. The fourth border was similar to No. 3, but omitting the heddle combination 1 and 2.

Note in this sample the good effect produced by lines of varying widths to outline each patterned border.

167

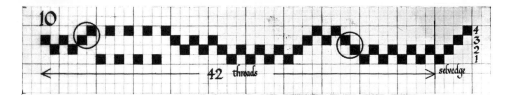

10

42 threads   selvedge

4
3
2
1

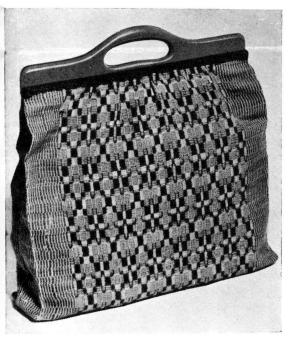

FIG. 150.

FIG. 151.

10. *Trellis* (42 threads).— Twenty-three threads for the last repeat. The bag, Fig. 150, was woven from this draft on a mercerised cotton warp (28 threads per inch) with a thin 2-ply wool in a colour to match the warp for the binder, and a thicker 2-ply wool in a contrasting colour for the weft.

The sampler tray cloth, Fig. 151, was woven from the same draft. Note that in *weaving* the 'accidentals' 2 and 3 at the beginning, and 3 and 4 at the end (shown in brackets) have been omitted, thus giving a more defined pattern.

Woven as follows:

8 rows raising heddles 1 and 2
6 ,, ,, ,, 3 ,, 4
8 ,, ,, ,, 1 ,, 2
6 ,, ,, ,, 2 ,, 3
8 ,, ,, ,, 1 ,, 4
6 ,, ,, ,, 2 ,, 3

The cloth has been folded over to show both sides.

11. Clematis.

11. *Clematis* (46 threads).—For the last pattern use only the first thirty-nine threads.

The illustration shows both sides of a piece of fabric woven from this draft.

In order to produce the pattern the heddles are tied as follows:

Pedals				Heddles
1	–	–	–	1 and 2
2	–	–	–	2 and 3
3	–	–	–	1 and 3
4	–	–	–	2 and 4
5	–	–	–	3 and 4
6	–	–	–	1 and 4

The pedals are worked as follows:

		Pedal
*2 rows on		2
2 ,,		5
6 ,,		6
2 ,,		1
2 ,,		2
2 ,,		5
*6 ,,		2

Repeat from * to * in the opposite direction to complete the pattern, ending with two rows on 2

FIG. 152.

FIG. 153.

169

12. *Dog Tracks* (36 threads).

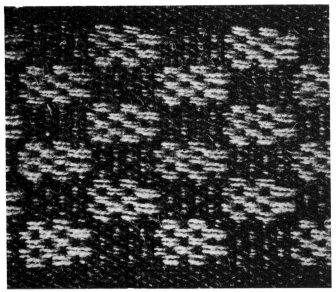

FIG. 154.

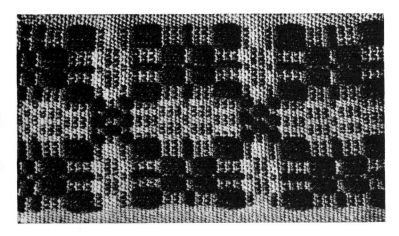

FIG. 155.

13. *Dog Tracks Adaptation* (20 threads).—The illustration shows the standard pattern woven from this draft.

14. *Sweet Briar Beauty* (38 threads).—It will require 29 extra threads in order to make the pattern balance at both edges.

This pattern is dealt with in great detail in Chapter XIV dealing with 'The Analysis of Woven Fabric' and Fig. 177 shows the order in which the heddles are used to produce it.

14. Sweet Briar Beauty.

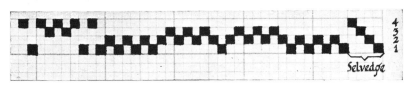

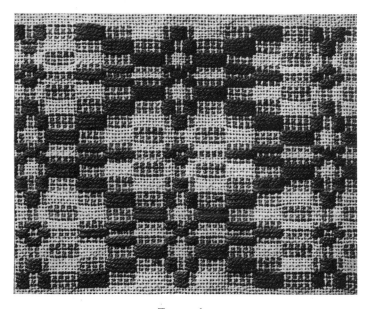

FIG. 156.

15. *Sea Star* (96 threads).—Woven as per draft. Sixty-seven extra threads required for a balanced pattern.

This sample was woven on 2-ply wool warp 14 dents to 1 inch with a 2-ply wool for binder, 3-ply wool for the pattern.

The pattern was produced on a table loom—the heddles being used in the following order:

    4 rows on each of the following:—1 and 2; 2 and 3; 3 and 4.
      (two heddles used together)

2	,,	,,	,,	2 and 3; 1 and 2; 2 and 3.
4	,,	,,	,,	3 and 4; 2 and 3; 1 and 2; 1 and 4.
2	,,	,,	,,	1 and 2; 2 and 3.

      The pattern was reversed from this point.

171

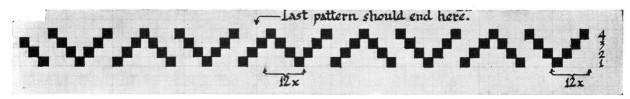

12x   12x   4 3 2 1

16. Polish Towel.

FIG. 157

16. *Polish Towel* (150 threads, including all repeats).—This combines goose eye and diagonal weave, and is suitable for cotton or linen; no binder required. The last pattern should end as indicated on the draft.

172

4
3
2
1
Selvedge.

17. Domino Sixes.

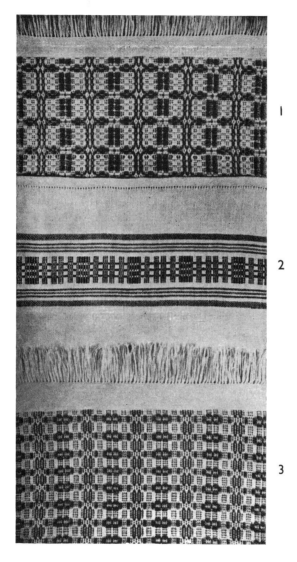

1

2

3

FIG. 158.

17. *Domino Sixes* (60 threads).—In order to get a balanced pattern only 17 threads will be required in the last repeat.

Fig. 158. *Sample* 1 was woven with double weft for the pattern on a table loom as follows:

173

2 rows raising heddles 1 and 2
4 ,, ,, ,, 1 ,, 4
2 ,, ,, ,, 1 ,, 2
*2 ,, ,, ,, 2 ,, 3
2 ,, ,, ,, 3 ,, 4
2 ,, ,, ,, 2 ,, 3
4 ,, ,, ,, 1 ,, 2
2 ,, ,, ,, 1 ,, 4
4 ,, ,, ,, 1 ,, 2
2 ,, ,, ,, 1 ,, 4
4 ,, ,, ,, 1 ,, 2*

The section * to * was repeated eight times and then continued as follows:

2 rows raising heddles 2 and 3
2 ,, ,, ,, 3 ,, 4
2 ,, ,, ,, 2 ,, 3
2 ,, ,, ,, 1 ,, 2
2 ,, ,, ,, 1 ,, 4
2 ,, ,, ,, 1 ,, 2

Sample 2 (Tray Cloth) was produced as follows:

6 rows raising heddles 1 and 2
2 ,, ,, ,, 3 ,, 4
4 ,, ,, ,, 1 ,, 2
2 ,, ,, ,, 3 ,, 4
4 ,, ,, ,, 1 ,, 2
2 ,, ,, ,, 3 ,, 4
6 ,, ,, ,, 1 ,, 2

Sample 3 (Mat) produced as follows:

4 rows raising heddles 1 and 2
2 ,, ,, ,, 1 ,, 4
4 ,, ,, ,, 3 ,, 4
2 ,, ,, ,, 1 ,, 4
6 ,, ,, ,, 1 ,, 2
2 ,, ,, ,, 1 ,, 4
4 ,, ,, ,, 3 ,, 4
2 ,, ,, ,, 1 ,, 4

18. Solomon's Delight.

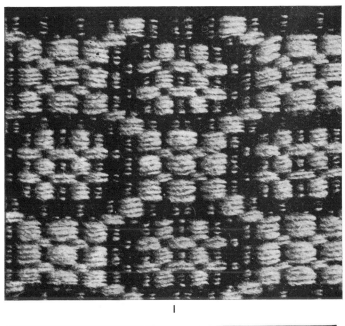

1

2

FIG. 159.

18. *Solomon's Delight* (40 threads).—Twenty-seven extra threads required to balance the pattern. Fig. 159 (Nos. 1 and 2) shows a piece of fabric woven from this draft. Two-and-a-half repeats of the pattern have been woven in width and depth.

A coarser wool has here been used for the pattern which enables the binder thread to be packed more closely.

175

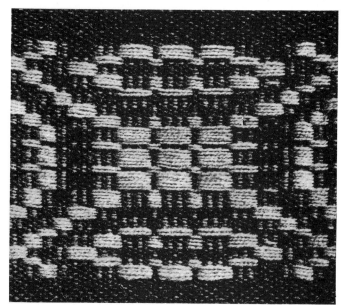

Fig. 160.

Fig. 161.

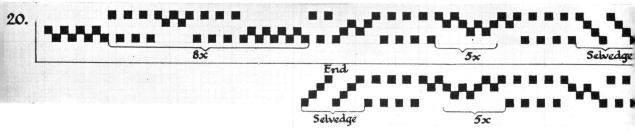

176

19. *Maltese Cross* (78 threads).—Three extra threads required to balance the pattern. A piece of fabric woven in accordance with the threading draft is shown in Fig. 160. Only one repeat of the pattern has been woven. A binder thread of single spun wool and in a contrasting colour from the warp has been used, which enables the weft to be closely packed.

20. *Block pattern* for cushion square with border. This can be woven on table or foot-power loom as follows:

Foot-Power Loom		Table Loom (Heddles raised)	Table Loom (Heddles lowered)
12 rows	Pedal 1	2 and 3	1 and 4
8 ,,	2	1 ,, 2	3 ,, 4
8 ,,	5	1 ,, 4	2 ,, 3
8 ,,	2	1 ,, 2	3 ,, 4
8 ,,	5	1 ,, 4	2 ,, 3
8 ,,	2	1 ,, 2	3 ,, 4
8 ,,	5	1 ,, 4	2 ,, 3
8 ,,	2	1 ,, 2	3 ,, 4
10 ,,	1	2 ,, 3	1 ,, 4
6 ,,	5	1 ,, 4	2 ,, 3
10 ,,	1	2 ,, 3	1 ,, 4

End of border.

Centre of Cushion

*12 rows	6	3 and 4	1 and 2
10 ,,	1	2 ,, 3	1 ,, 4
6 ,,	5	1 ,, 4	2 ,, 3
*10 ,,	1	2 ,, 3	1 ,, 4

Repeat * 9 times.

	Heddles	Heddles
Then 12 rows on Pedal 6.	3 and 4	1 and 2

Then Border repeated in the reverse direction.

177

21. *Cleveland Web* (46 threads).—Twenty-five extra threads required for a balanced pattern.

FIG. 162.

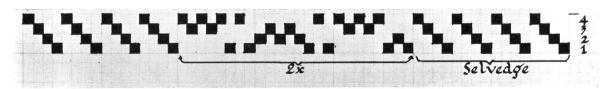

22. Cleveland Web Adaptation.

22. *Cleveland Web Adaptation* (48 threads).—The illustration (Fig. 162) shows a strip of material woven from this draft. The sixteen selvedge threads give an interesting border on either side of the pattern. The draft is given for this as it was woven. It would be improved by reversing the threading order of the left-hand selvedge, and adding three extra threads to balance the pattern.

This pattern was produced by using the threading draft as the treadling draft. Another adaptation of the Cleveland Web is shown in Fig. 102 on the four-heddle Box Loom and details for producing this pattern are given in the same chapter.

178

23.

FIG. 163.

FIG. 164.

Section of scarf woven by girl of 14.

23. *Honeysuckle* (26 threads).—Seven extra threads to balance the pattern. This is one of the most popular drafts and is dealt with in great detail in Chapter XI.

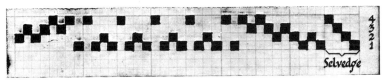

24. Butternut.

FIG. 165.

24. *Butternut.*—With 36 threads to the pattern, is useful for cushions, runners and similar articles. The section of the sampler illustrated shows a variety of patterns produced from this draft. Three extra threads are needed to balance the pattern.

25. Snail Trail.

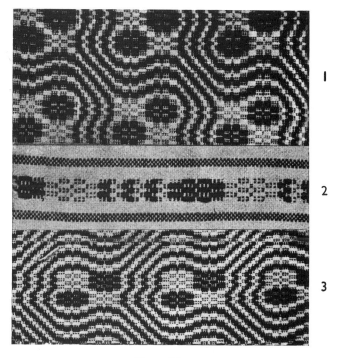

FIG. 166.

25. *Snail Trail* (92 threads).—As this is such a popular pattern, full directions are given for weaving it as shown in No. 1. The sampler was woven on a table loom in accordance with the threading draft, but slight variations were made in the number of rows of weft for each pattern combination.

Foot-Power Loom: (Heddles lowered by pedal to which they are attached)			Table Loom: (Heddles raised)		
		Heddles			*Heddles*
(1) 4 rows lowering	..	3 and 4	(1) 4 rows raising	..	1 and 2
3 ,, ,,	..	1 ,, 4	3 ,, ,,	..	2 ,, 3
2 ,, ,,	..	3 ,, 4	2 ,, ,,	..	1 ,, 2
3 ,, ,,	..	1 ,, 4	3 ,, ,,	..	2 ,, 3
4 ,, ,,	..	3 ,, 4	4 ,, ,,	..	1 ,, 2

181

	Heddles			*Heddles*
(2) 4 rows lowering ..	2 ,, 3	(2) 4 rows raising ..	1 ,, 4
3 ,, ,, ..	1 ,, 2	3 ,, ,, ..	3 ,, 4
2 ,, ,, ..	2 ,, 3	2 ,, ,, ..	1 ,, 4
3 ,, ,, ..	1 ,, 2	3 ,, ,, ..	3 ,, 4
4 ,, ,, ..	2 ,, 3	4 ,, ,, ..	1 ,, 4
(3) 3 ,, ,, ..	3 ,, 4	(3) 3 ,, ,, ..	1 ,, 2
2 ,, ,, ..	1 ,, 4	2 ,, ,, ..	2 ,, 3
3 ,, ,, ..	1 ,, 2	3 ,, ,, ..	3 ,, 4
2 ,, ,, ..	2 ,, 3	2 ,, ,, ..	1 ,, 4
3 ,, ,, ..	3 ,, 4	3 ,, ,, ..	1 ,, 2
2 ,, ,, ..	1 ,, 4	2 ,, ,, ..	2 ,, 3
3 ,, ,, ..	1 ,, 2	3 ,, ,, ..	3 ,, 4
2 ,, ,, ..	2 ,, 3	2 ,, ,, ..	1 ,, 4
3 ,, ,, ..	3 ,, 4	3 ,, ,, ..	1 ,, 2
2 ,, ,, ..	1 ,, 4	2 ,, ,, ..	2 ,, 3
3 ,, ,, ..	1 ,, 2	3 ,, ,, ..	3 ,, 4
2 ,, ,, ..	2 ,, 3	2 ,, ,, ..	1 ,, 4
Then repeat 1, 2 and 3		Then repeat 1, 2 and 3	

The piece of material woven from this threading draft does not show the pattern to advantage. It is a large all-over pattern and suitable for bags, cushions, etc. If a wool weft is used on a mercerised cotton warp (28 threads to the inch) a good firm fabric is produced, which is most suitable for work bags, cushions and other furnishing fabrics.

If woven in accordance with the threading draft the pattern begins with the blocks, but for a cushion a more pleasing effect is produced if the scrolls are woven first. This necessitates using that section of the draft which is shown in a bracket and marked 3X first, and then weaving from the beginning of the draft to the end, and repeating as often as required, ending with the scrolls for the other border.

An interesting effect can be given to the two selvedges of a cushion by repeating the threading of the selvedge threads several times—entering them in their correct order. This effect is shown on the bag, Fig. 150. The small border, No. 2, was also woven from this draft. A table loom was used and the heddles were raised in the following order:

2 rows using heddles 1 and 2
2 ,, ,, ,, 2 ,, 3
2 ,, ,, ,, 1 ,, 2
2 ,, ,, ,, 2 ,, 3
2 ,, ,, ,, 1 ,, 2

No. 3 shows another variation of the original pattern.

182

26.

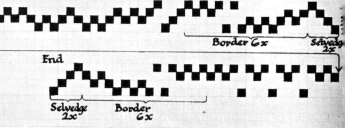

Border 6x   Selvedge 2x

End

Selvedge 2x   Border 6x

26. Adaptation of Windflower

FIG. 167.

26. *Adaptation of Windflower.* Suitable for cushions, curtains, etc. It consists of a border of 16 threads on either side, repeated six times (which can be increased or decreased to suit individual taste) and a pattern of 73 threads repeated as many times as the width of the material necessitates. In order to make a balanced pattern, an extra 30 threads must be added after threading the last complete pattern.

183

As the last thread of the pattern is in heddle 3 and the first thread of the pattern in heddle 3, an extra thread should be added on heddle 4 *at the beginning of each repeat of the pattern*: otherwise the tabby weave would be upset if two threads passed through adjacent heddles on the same heddle frame.

The cushion, Fig. 167, was woven on a cotton warp with 24 threads to the inch. The number of warp threads was calculated as follows:

First border (5 repeats)	80 threads
Second border	80 ,,
First pattern	73 ,,
Two repeats of pattern (74 threads each) ..	148 ,,
Part pattern (for balance)	30 ,,
Two selvedges (8 threads each)	16 ,,
Extra thread to make an even number for warping	1 ,,
Total	428 ,,

NOTE: If threads are warped in pairs an extra thread can be added (to make an even number) to this or any other pattern. This should be put through the heddle with the last thread of the border or, if no border, with the last thread of the pattern.

A foot-power loom should be tied as follows:

Pedal		Heddles
1	to	2 and 3
2	to	1 ,, 2
3	to	1 ,, 3
4	to	2 ,, 4
5	to	1 ,, 4
6	to	3 ,, 4

The cushion was woven on a foot-power loom as follows:

Selvedge : 1 row using Pedal 2
           1 ,, ,, ,, 1
           1 ,, ,, ,, 6
           1 ,, ,, ,, 5

Border : 4 rows using Pedal 2 ⎤ Repeat four times
         4 ,, ,, ,, 1 ⎥ (this can be varied
         4 ,, ,, ,, 6 ⎥ to suit the individual
         4 ,, ,, ,, 5 ⎥ taste)

Pattern : *1 row using Pedal 2 ⎥
          1 ,, ,, ,, 1 ⎥
          1 ,, ,, ,, 6 ⎦

1	row	using	Pedal	5	
4	,,	,,	,,	2	
4	,,	,,	,,	1	
2	,,	,,	,,	2	
4	,,	,,	,,	1	Repeat * to * 4 times
4	,,	,,	,,	2	
1	,,	,,	,,	5	
1	,,	,,	,,	6	
1	,,	,,	,,	1	
2	,,	,,	,,	2	
1	,,	,,	,,	1	
1	,,	,,	,,	6	*

Then :

1	row	using	Pedal	5	
1	,,	,,	,,	6	
1	,,	,,	,,	1	
1	,,	,,	,,	2	
4	,,	,,	,,	5	
2	,,	,,	,,	6	
2	,,	,,	,,	5	
2	,,	,,	,,	6	
2	,,	,,	,,	1	
2	,,	,,	,,	6	
4	,,	,,	,,	1	
2	,,	,,	,,	6	
2	,,	,,	,,	1	
2	,,	,,	,,	6	
2	,,	,,	,,	5	
2	,,	,,	,,	6	
4	,,	,,	,,	5	
1	,,	,,	,,	2	
1	,,	,,	,,	1	
1	,,	,,	,,	6	
1	,,	,,	,,	5	

Then repeat first part of pattern from * to * four times; border four times, then selvedge once—all in reverse order.

NOTE: The black cord put in the weaving when on the loom, to be withdrawn as the hemstitching is done. This does away with the necessity of drawing out threads from the weaving when finished.

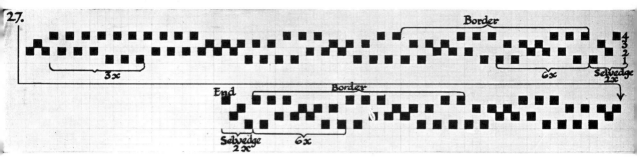

27. Orange Peel.

FIG. 168.

27. *Orange Peel* (264 threads).—An attractive pattern suitable for covers and curtains. Draft given with border suitable for cushion top, as illustrated. If a narrower border is required, one or more repeats of the threads shown in brackets should be omitted.

Note that the same method of threading the selvedge is adopted as in the Chariot Wheel No. 29. This means that heddles 1 and 2; 3 and 4 are used for the tabby weaving.

The cushion was woven on a beige mercerised cotton warp 28 threads to the inch with a fine beige Botany wool warp for the tabby weave (weft) and various colours of mercerised cotton for the pattern.

The cushion was woven as follows:

1 in. plain beige tabby.

Border :

2 rows using heddles 1 and 4⌉
1 ,, ,, ,, 2 ,, 4 | Repeat nine times. Shades of rust,
2 ,, ,, ,, 2 ,, 3 | orange, yellow.
1 ,, ,, ,, 1 ,, 3⌋

Then:

*4 rows using heddles 1 and 4   Blue-green pattern with brown tabby.
2 ,, ,, ,, 1 ,, 3⌉
1 ,, ,, ,, 2 ,, 3 |
2 ,, ,, ,, 2 ,, 4 | Rust pattern with beige tabby.
1 ,, ,, ,, 1 ,, 4 |
3 ,, ,, ,, 1 ,, 3 |
2 ,, ,, ,, 2 ,, 3⌋

Then Blocks:

3 rows using heddles 2 and 4   (first block orange)
3 ,, ,, ,, 1 ,, 4   (second block rust)
3 ,, ,, ,, 2 ,, 4   (orange)
3 ,, ,, ,, 1 ,, 4   (rust)
3 ,, ,, ,, 2 ,, 4   (orange)
3 ,, ,, ,, 1 ,, 4   (rust)
3 ,, ,, ,, 2 ,, 4   (orange)

Then:

3 rows using heddles 2 and 3
2 ,, ,, ,, 1 ,, 3
2 ,, ,, ,, 1 ,, 4
1 ,, ,, ,, 2 ,, 4
2 ,, ,, ,, 2 ,, 3
1 ,, ,, ,, 1 ,, 3* end of pattern.

Repeat from * to * as many times as desired.

Then four rows using heddles 1 and 4 (green).

Then second border is reached and should be woven in reverse, using the same colours as for the first border.

NOTE: If woven on a table loom the pattern as photographed will be on the underside of the work.

28.

28. Whig Rose.

FIG. 169.

28. *Whig Rose* can be used as an all-over pattern for cushions, etc., or with an added border for runners, curtains, mats, etc.

The small mat shown in Fig. 169 has a border and the pattern draft has been adapted to suit one complete motif.

Selvedge : 8 threads; 1 2 3 4; 1 2 3 4 (reading from right to left).

Right Border : 35 threads: 3 2; 3 4 3 4; 1 4 1; 4 3 4 3; 2 3; 2 1 2; 3 2: 3 4 3 4; 1 4; 1 2 1 2; 3; 2 1 2 1 (reading from right to left).

188

Pattern : 103 threads.

NOTE: The first and last threads of the pattern must be adjusted to fit in with the border threads; therefore the first thread given in the pattern draft should be omitted. The draft should then be followed to the end and two additional threads added, 2, 1 (reading from right to left) before starting to thread the second border.

Left Border : 35 threads: 1 2 1 2; 3; 2 1 2 1; 4 1; 4 3 4 3; 2 3; 2 1 2; 3 2; 3 4 3 4; 1 4 1; 4 3 4 3; 2 3 (reading from right to left).

Selvedge : 8 threads: 1 2 3 4; 1 2 3 4 (reading from right to left).

The mat was woven as follows:

2 rows using heddles 1 and 2
2 ,, ,, ,, 2 ,, 3
2 ,, ,, ,, 3 ,, 4
2 ,, ,, ,, 1 ,, 4
4 ,, ,, ,, 1 ,, 2
2 ,, ,, ,, 2 ,, 3

Then:

4 rows using heddles 1 and 4
4 ,, ,, ,, 3 ,, 4
4 ,, ,, ,, 2 ,, 3
4 ,, ,, ,, 1 ,, 2
4 ,, ,, ,, 2 ,, 3
4 ,, ,, ,, 3 ,, 4
4 ,, ,, ,, 1 ,, 4

Then:

6 rows using heddles 1 and 2
4 ,, ,, ,, 2 ,, 3
2 ,, ,, ,, 1 ,, 2 } Small block in each of the four corners
4 ,, ,, ,, 2 ,, 3
6 ,, ,, ,, 1 ,, 2

Then:

8 rows using heddles 1 and 4
8 ,, ,, ,, 3 ,, 4
4 ,, ,, ,, 1 ,, 4
4 ,, ,, ,, 3 ,, 4 This is the centre, and from this point the mat should now be woven from the instructions in reverse.

The number of rows indicated can be reduced, e.g. to the 8 6 rows and the 6 to 4 rows. This would be an improvement as it would make the pattern more circular and less elongated.

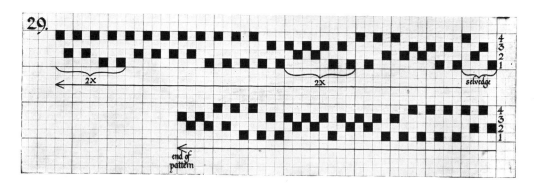

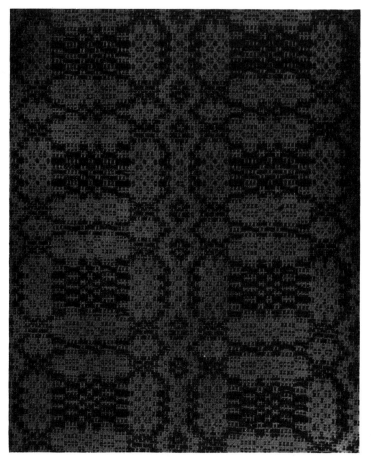

FIG. 170.

29. *Adaptation of the Chariot Wheel* with 96 threads.—The number of threads in the original pattern has been reduced by omitting many of the repeats on each combination. Other adaptations can be made in the same way. On looking at the pattern draft it will be noticed that the selvedge threads are entered in the following order, 1, 3, 2, 4, which is contrary to the usual pro-

cedure. This means that heddles 1 and 2 and 3 and 4 will be used for the tabby weaving and should therefore be tied to the two middle pedals. It makes no difference in the operation of the loom which pair of heddles is tied to each pedal, but they are generally tied in the following order:

Heddles				Pedals	
1 and 4	–	–	–	1	
2 ,, 3	–	–	–	2	
1 ,, 3	–	–	–	3	plain weaving
2 ,, 4	–	–	–	4	
1 ,, 2	–	–	–	5	
3 ,, 4	–	–	–	6	

For this draft and that for Orange Peel, No. 27, the heddles should be tied as follows:

Heddles				Pedals	
1 and 3	–	–	–	1	
2 ,, 3	–	–	–	2	
1 ,, 2	–	–	–	3	Tabby
3 ,, 4	–	–	–	4	
1 ,, 4	–	–	–	5	
2 ,, 4	–	–	–	6	

Attention is drawn to this point and to drafts given for this method of entering the threads so that a weaver can make herself thoroughly familiar with either method, and thus be able to use any draft with ease.

Should a weaver, however, be using a draft from a book, she must be careful to see that her method of tying the heddles is the same as that given in the book, otherwise the treadling draft would have to be altered, e.g. if the book gives heddles 2 and 3 to No. 1 pedal, and the worker ties 2 and 3 to No. 2 pedal, then when the book says use pedal 1, meaning the one which pulls down heddles 2 and 3, the worker must use No. 2 pedal, and so on.

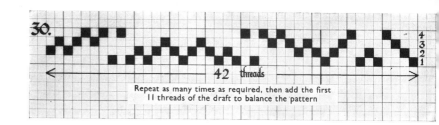

42 threads

Repeat as many times as required, then add the first
II threads of the draft to balance the pattern

30. *California.* — This pattern draft was evolved from a small scrap of material sent by a weaver from abroad, and as its name was unknown, the writer called it 'California'. It is similar to a miniature Maltese Cross and is a most attractive pattern, both for borders, runners, curtains, etc., and for all-over patterns (see below). Many other interesting all-over patterns can be produced from this draft.

Fig. 171*a*. This pattern was produced by following the directions indicated on the large draft, Fig. 178.

Fig. 171*b*. This shows an adaptation of Fig. 178 which makes an attractive all-over pattern.

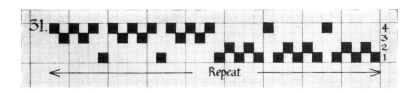

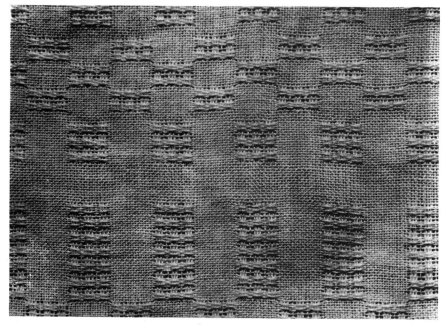

FIG. 172

31. *Swedish Lace or Bronson Weave.*—This is a most interesting type of weaving. It is suitable for curtains, table mats, stoles, etc., and is a pleasant change from the usual overshot patterns.

The illustration shows a section of a table napkin made on a mercerised cotton warp (24 threads per inch) with linen weft. For this type of weaving it is advisable to use a tightly spun yarn, keeping the warp very taut while weaving and beating the weft lightly in order to retain the lacey effect. The weaving can be made still more lacey by omitting one or more dents in the reed after each group of five threads, and experiments can be made alternating the arrangement of the lacey stripes with the plain stripes or in making the whole centre of a cloth or napkin in lace weave, with the plain border all round. The authors recommend all weavers, having once grasped the principle of this type of weaving, to experiment and to draft their own patterns.

The tie-up for this weave is as follows:

Heddles		Pedals
1	to	1
1 and 3	to	2
2 ,, 4	to	3
4	to	4

The pedals were used in the following order (from right to left).

3, 1, 3, 1, 3 (2) 3, 1, 3, 1, 3. Repeat as desired.

Then: 2, 4, 2, 4, 2 (3) 2, 4, 2, 4, 2. Repeat as desired.

193

FIG. 173.

FIG. 173*a*.

Tea cosy woven in varying colours on a peach mercerised cotton warp.

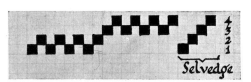

Selvedge

32 (1). *Honeycomb Pattern* (16 threads).—For the pattern the tie-up is as follows :

Heddles			Pedals
1	–	–	1
2	–	–	2
3	–	–	3
4	–	–	4

Pattern 1 gives the most interesting tweed effect if the pedals are used in the order 4, 3, 2, 1.

For the Honeycomb Pattern 2, the pedals are used as follows:

1 then 2 four times, using fine thread.

1 and 3 pressed down together once. Coarse thread.

3 then 4 four times. Fine thread.

2 and 4 pressed down together once. Coarse thread.

For a Six-Pedal Loom the tie-up for Honeycomb Pattern 2 is as follows:

Heddles		Pedals
1	to	1
2	to	2
1 and 3	to	3
2 ,, 4	to	4
3	to	5
4	to	6

The sample was woven with fine bouclé and thick single-spun wool, on a warp with 16 threads per inch, as follows:

1 row coarse thread using pedal 3.

4 rows fine thread using pedals 2 and 1 alternately.

1 row coarse thread using pedal 4.

4 rows fine thread using pedals 5 and 6 alternately.

194

A few more pattern drafts (not illustrated) will now be given.

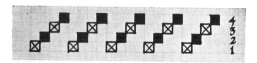

33. *Double Weave two-colour Fabric.*
Details for this type of weaving are given fully in Chapter XI.

34. *Betsy Ross* (47 threads).—The heddles should be tied as follows:

Pedals			Heddles
1	–	–	1 and 2
2	–	–	2 ,, 3
3	–	–	1 ,, 3
4	–	–	2 ,, 4
5	–	–	3 ,, 4
6	–	–	1 ,, 4

A variety of small borders can be woven from this draft, e.g.:

(1) Pedals 3, 6, 4, 5, four times.
(2) ,, 1 and 5, eight times.
(3) ,, 6, 3, 6, 2, 6, 2, 6, 3.
(4) ,, 4, 6, 3, 2, four times.

The pattern should be threaded up a definite number of times—the last six threads being omitted at the end.

35. *Diamond Adaptation* (20 threads).—Suitable for articles in linen.

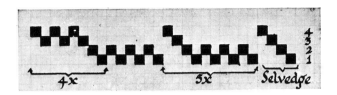

36. *Sugar Loaf* (88 threads).

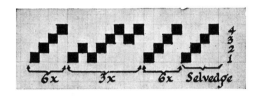

37. *Norway Towel* (72 threads).—Another interesting pattern, suitable for runners, towels, tablecloths, etc.

38. *Quadrille* (70 threads).—For a balanced pattern only 19 threads required for the last repeat.

39. *Sun, Moon and Stars* (126 threads).

40. *Solomon's Seal* (68 threads).—An extra 47 threads required for a balanced pattern.

196

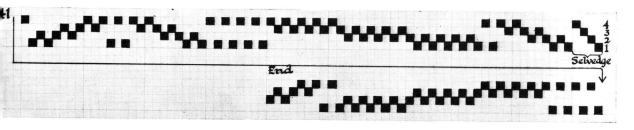

41. *Star of Bethlehem* (116 threads).—Woven as per draft. Three extra threads to balance.

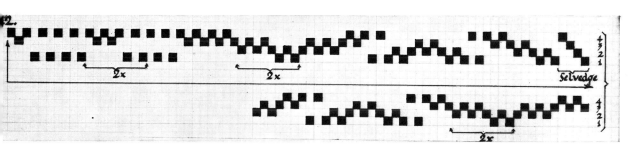

42. *Lovers' Knot* (140 threads).

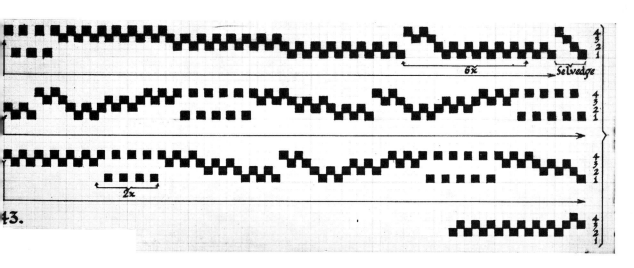

43. *Pine Bloom* (330 threads).—A most attractive pattern suitable for covers.

FIG. 174.

FIG. 175.

44. *Check Scarf* (Fig. 174).—Thread two black, two white threads alternately through heddles 1, 2, 3, 4 (reading from right to left).

Foot-Power Loom : Tie heddles 1 and 3 to Pedal 1
                 ,,   ,,   2 and 4   ,,   2

Weave alternately two rows black, two white, using pedal 1, then pedal 2. Repeat.

The same effect can be produced on a loom with a rigid heddle or on an ordinary waist loom. Thread two black, two white threads alternately (one through a hole in the rigid heddle and the next through a slit).

Weave alternately two rows black, two white. Repeat. This is an effective pattern for the early stages of weaving.

45. *Check Scarf* (Fig. 175). Woven on table loom. Warp : Four black, four white threads alternately, through heddles 4, 3, 2, 1 (reading from right to left). Weft : Four rows black, four white.

Border : (*a*) Weave 1 row raising heddle 4 using white

,,	1	,,	,,	,,	3	,,	,,
,,	1	,,	,,	,,	2	,,	,,
,,	1	,,	,,	,,	1	,,	,,

(*b*)   ,,   1   ,,   ,,   heddles 432 together using black

,,	1	,,	,,	,,	431	,,	,,	,,
,,	1	,,	,,	,,	421	,,	,,	,,
,,	1	,,	,,	,,	321	,,	,,	,,

The body of the scarf was woven entirely with white weft as follows :

	1 row raising heddle	4
1	,,	,,	,,	3
1	,,	,,	,,	2
1	,,	,,	,,	1
1	,,	,,	,,	2
1	,,	,,	,,	3
1	,,	,,	,,	4

Repeat.

NOTE : In the second part of the pattern (*b*) the weaver may find that instead of raising three heddles each time it might be easier to raise all four heddles at the start and then lower one heddle as required. Thus, for the first row heddle 1 would be lowered, heddle 2 for the second, heddle 3 for the third, and heddle 4 for the fourth row.

CHAPTER XIV
The Analysis of Woven Fabric

AFTER some experience in weaving on a foot-power loom from given threading drafts, a weaver cannot fail to be interested in the reverse process, the analysis of woven fabrics.

In order to do this, a sheet of ordinary graph paper, on which four lines can be drawn to represent the four heddles, must be available. The previous experience in drafting patterns from a given threading draft will be an aid to this next stage—the writing of a threading draft from a woven pattern.

From experience a weaver will be familiar with the following principles underlying four-heddle weaving:

1. There are two combinations for plain weaving: 1 and 3; 2 and 4 are more usual, though 1 and 2; 3 and 4 are sometimes used for the tabby weave. The former method will in this case be adopted. Each pattern row is followed by a row of tabby weave.

2. For pattern-weaving, four combinations are possible, viz.:

1 and 2

2 ,, 3

3 ,, 4

1 ,, 4

3. All colour blocks in both horizontal and vertical lines are made by the same heddle combination.

4. The first thread of one block of colour is usually the last of a previous block.

It is advisable to select a fairly simple pattern with bold blocks of colour for a first experiment in pattern analysis. Fig. 176 shows a strip of weaving (done by a child of twelve years of age) from the Sweet Briar Beauty threading draft, whilst Fig. 177 shows the same strip drafted on graph paper.

It will be obvious from previous experience in using the threading draft as the treadling draft that an error has been made in weaving blocks A and B (see Fig. 176). The threading draft, indicates eight rows of weft for blocks both A and B using heddles 1 and 2, whereas six rows have been woven on Block A and eight on Block B. (This error is, of course, quite obvious on the drafted pattern, Fig. 177.) The unit of design must be picked out. In this case it consists of a rectangle CD, D¹, C¹. A diagonal should be indicated on the fabric by a line of pins or a tacking thread in white cotton from top right-hand corner to bottom left-hand corner D¹. (In wheel patterns a line is often drawn from the centre of one pattern to the centre of another.)

200

FIG. 176.—'SWEET BRIAR BEAUTY'.

Begin at corner C with first block of colour marked 1. Decide on the first heddle combination for this block, e.g. 1 and 2; count the number of threads in the block (8 in this case), and write or draft out on squared paper: 21212121.

Block of colour No. 2 in draft must next be taken and the threads counted(7).

In accordance with principle four, the first thread of block 2 may be the last thread of block 1. The last thread of block 1 is 2, and the next heddle combination used should contain 2. Reference to principle 2, the only other heddle combination possible is 2 and 3, so the draft for blocks 1 and 2 is written: (2)32323(2)1212121, reading from right to left. (The last thread of block 1, which is also the first of block 2, is indicated by a ring to avoid confusion.) Block 3 is taken next, and it is found to consist of three threads, of which (2) is the first. This means that heddle combination 2 and 1 is used. The draft now reads:

(2)1(2)32323(2)1212121

Block 4 is considered next, and consists of seven threads, beginning with 2. Heddle combination 2 and 3 must be used, as, according to principle 3, all vertical blocks are made by the same heddle combination. (Blocks 4 and 2 are obviously made by the same combination.) The draft now reads:

(2)32323(2)1(2)32323(2)1212121

Block 5 has eight threads, the first of which should be 2. This block is made by the same heddle combination as block 1 (which is 2 and 1), so the draft now reads:

(1)212121(2)32323(2)1(2)32323(2)1212121

Block 6 has four threads, of which 1 is the first. According to principle 2, the only other heddle combination possible is 1 and 4. The draft now reads:

(4)14(1)212121(2)32323(2)1(2)32323(2)1212121

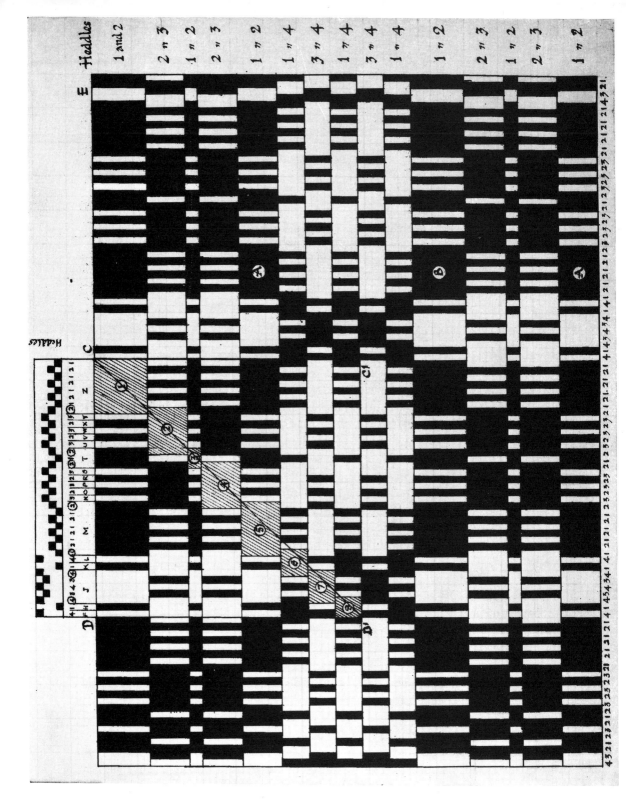

Block 7 has five threads, of which 4 is the first. The heddle combination used must be 3 and 4, so the draft now reads:

(4)343(4)14(1)212121(2)32323(2)1(2)32323(2)1212121

Block 8 has four threads, of which the first thread is 4, so heddle combination 1 and 4 must next be used.

On the line from D to bottom row of block 8 it will be seen that the last thread of block 8 is really the first thread of the block which begins the next repeat of the pattern; therefore only three threads should be drafted in block 8, making 38 threads for the pattern. The complete draft is:

(4)1(4)343(4)14(1)212121(2)32323(2)1(2)32323(2)1212121

It will be seen that blocks 7 and 8 have been repeated in the sampler, though not indicated in the original draft No. 14. These blocks and any other sections of the pattern can be repeated as often as desired without affecting the draft.

For this reason the base of rectangle CD, D¹, C¹ on the sampler is taken in line with the bottom row of block 8, as this includes each section of the woven pattern.

The threading draft taken from a piece of fabric may be not identical with the original one for the particular pattern under consideration, owing to the variation in the heddle combination chosen for the first block of colour, e.g. heddle combination 3 and 4 might have been chosen for block 1; in which case the order of the whole threading draft would have been altered. The details of the fabric woven from this draft, however, would remain the same, and could easily be checked if drafted on paper.

Another equally accurate method of analysing pattern, which is particularly useful for simple straightforward patterns similar to Monk's Belt and Rosepath, will now be described.

Referring again to the 'Sweet Briar Beauty' Sampler (Fig. 176 and Fig. 177), the unit of design (which is repeated) will be picked out on the top row of the pattern. This is between C and D or C and E, and can be marked on the sampler with pins.

Each group of threads (whether up or down) on the sampler is lettered on the draft (see Fig. 177), and when a letter is mentioned, it will refer to the particular group of threads as indicated on the draft.

Z. Heddle combination 1 and 2 will be taken for this group of eight threads (all threads on these heddles being pulled down).

Draft for this group (reading from right to left in each case) will be 21212121.

Y. This thread is up, and must be either 3 or 4. Principle 2 states that 1 and 3, 2 and 4 are heddle combinations for tabby weave. This means that alternate threads are on either heddles 1 and 3, or 2 and 4.

FIG. 178 —THREADING DRAFT. 'CALIFORNIA'.

204

As 2 is the last thread on block Z, 3 must be the next thread (if 4 were substituted for this it would disturb the tabby weave).

X. This thread is down, and must be either 2 or 1. As 1 cannot follow 3, the thread used must be 2.

W. One thread up (3).

V. One thread down (2).

U. One thread up (3).

T. Heddle combination used, 2 and 1.

As last thread used was 3, the first thread in this block must be 2. The draft for this block is: 212.

S. One thread up. This must be 3.

R. One thread down (2).

P. One thread up (3).

O. One thread down (2).

N. One thread up (3).

M. Eight threads down on heddle combination 1 and 2. As the last thread used was 3, the first one of this group must be 2, so the draft will read: 12121212.

L. One thread up (either 3 or 4). It must be 4 (as it follows 1).

K. One thread down, which must be 1.

J. Five threads up—heddle combination 3 and 4 (as this is the only combination not previously used). Draft for this block reads: 43434.

H. One thread down (1).

F. One thread up (4).

The whole draft can now be written from the figures given for each group of threads. This can also be used for the treadling draft, as explained in the previous chapter.

In this method it is only necessary to take any one pattern row horizontally for calculating the complete threading draft (the top row of pattern was analysed for convenience in this case).

This is possibly the simpler method. In the former method the complete woven pattern (which often covers many rows) has to be marked on the fabric. This sometimes presents difficulty to a beginner, particularly in the case of the more complicated patterns, e.g. some of the wheel patterns where one section of the pattern overlaps another.

The writer considers it a good plan for weavers, having worked out a draft as suggested in the second method, to mark on squared paper one or two complete repeats of the pattern as shown in Fig. 178 of the 'California' Draft. This makes a most useful piece of teaching apparatus as it shows so clearly the whole pattern and the number of threads (in this case eleven) required to balance the pattern.

After experience in the analysis of woven fabrics, the weaver can experiment in writing original threading drafts.

It is most interesting to use some of the traditional drafts but no weaver should be satisfied with merely copying and using ready-made drafts. The ultimate aim should be originality in the interpretation of a given draft and later the creating of original drafts for fabrics which weavers themselves want to use—remembering in every case that the woven fabric should be suitable for the purpose for which it is created.

Original drafts can be produced in one of two ways:

(1) In the purely mechanical way of planning on squared paper a draft, of which the alternate threads are on either heddles 1 and 3, or 2 and 4—these being the heddles used for the tabby weave. (The blocks of threads raised or pulled down together should not exceed six or eight in number as long weft threads passing over large groups of warp threads are loose and impracticable.)

or

(2) By the sounder and more intelligent method of planning on squared paper several repeats of a pleasing and interesting pattern and from these compiling a threading draft—still keeping in mind the important principles mentioned in the first method.

CHAPTER XV

Some Notes on Schemes of Work and Methods of Teaching

THE approach to weaving will vary with the type of school.

1. In a country school (or a town school where children may go for country holidays) children may collect fleece, and this will lead to an interest in spinning and washing, the collection of leaves, etc., for dyeing, and finally to weaving.

2. Some teachers may approach weaving through an interest in primitive man. This will bring weaving first, the invention of looms, and later spinning.

3. In an area where weaving is a staple industry the natural approach is through interest in the activities of the parents, and in the surrounding mills.

4. The craft may be approached merely from the point of view of finding occupation and allowing children of varying ages to make interesting and attractive articles suited to their ability.

Whichever mode of approach is adopted, the range of work suited to pupils of different ages may be generally taken to be as follows:

Infants.—Children of six and seven years of age may weave with paper, jute yarn, dyed tape, raffia, Turabast, knitting cotton, and coarse wool, on cardboard or on simple wooden frames. The work should be purposeful, that is, the children should always set out to make something—not merely to 'learn weaving'. They may make mats, kettle-holders, bags, needle-cases, etc. Colours used should be bright and pure.

After a little experience children may design striped patterns in cut paper work prior to weaving.

Juniors.—Similar work to the above, but of gradually improving quality. They may design plaid and simple all-over patterns to be woven in with needle or shuttle. They may discover for themselves or be encouraged to use a ruler or warp stick as a labour-saving device. They may do some spinning on simple spindles and experiment with dyeing with materials they can collect. They must now be encouraged to think of further labour-saving devices, and should be interested in the historical associations.

The 'rigid heddle' as a waist loom or used on a frame is the ideal apparatus for children at this stage, and they may make ties, belts, scarves, braids, and trimmings, and also a variety of useful articles made up from these strips. The material used will be 4- or 3-ply wool, or thick cotton, and the children should have access to a large variety of bright colours.

Leashes and leash rods may be introduced to the older children, but only for tabby weaving. Pattern will therefore be limited to stripes and plaids, and such simple decoration as can be woven in with heddle or shuttle. Some simple rug-weaving may be done—with strips of felt on a simple frame with no labour-saving devices or by making use of the rigid heddle loom. Both flat woven rugs and pile rugs may be made at this stage.

The Inkle loom may also be used; the former furnishing an opportunity for experience in warp patterns.

Seniors.—Spinning with spindles will continue and considerable skill may be acquired. The spinning wheel may now be introduced where possible. There should be further practice in dyeing—both with home-gathered and imported vegetable dyes; and notebooks should be kept, recording in great detail the type and quantity of the mordants and dyes used, and noting in particular the results obtained. A large variety of colours in the weaving materials should be available, including neutrals.

The question of labour-saving methods of weaving pattern now arises. This should at first be developed from the leash arrangement by fitting four sets of leashes to a loom previously used. Children should experiment on these and make on graph paper diagrams of their results.

When the pupils have discovered various twills and simple patterns, the teacher may introduce some of the simplest traditional 'thread-ups' and let the children make patterns from these, both on their looms and on paper. Since the leash type of loom is somewhat laborious, the pupils should soon be introduced to a simple four-heddle loom. They must now learn to make warps, preserving the crosses, and to thread up the loom. The first loom used will be small so that the children can quickly proceed to the actual weaving, and not be wearied by spending too long on the preparatory work.

Materials used will be wool (3- and 2-ply), with hand-spun wefts as far as possible; also cotton yarn, mercerised cotton and later possibly linen.

Some schools may find it possible to grow and prepare flax, others to keep Angora rabbits and use the combings for spinning and dyeing. All this is full of interest, and is excellent experience.

More difficult pattern drafts may now be introduced, and it will be found that senior girls soon become quite capable of independent work—and can plan an article, choose colours and pattern, make the warp, and thread up a loom without further help. Some of the pupils may like to do tapestry work—with coarse wool or thrums on a string warp to make small mats, stool tops, cushion covers, etc., or on a small scale with fine wool, silk or cotton to make small bags, pochettes, etc. The designing for this will be very valuable experience.

Tablet weaving will also provide very interesting work for pupils at this stage.

Given suitable equipment there need be no limit to the type of work undertaken by girls at the top of the Senior school, who should be allowed to follow individually the line which is of most interest to them.

With regard to the method of conducting the work, a few general hints may be given:

1. The work should be purposeful throughout, and involve thought on the part of the pupils. *What* the children produce is less important than the experience they gain in the process of production. The teacher who provides looms and tells or shows the children how to use them is depriving the activity of a great part of its value.

All pupils should have some experience of the simple type of loom, though they should not be kept too long on this type of work.

2. A few processes will have to be *taught*. They can usually be taught to a class or group by means of diagrams and practical demonstration, followed by careful individual help and supervision.

3. It is impossible to lay too much stress on the study of colour throughout a weaving course. Schools have made great progress in the *technique* of weaving during recent years, but the development of taste in the use of colour has not marched with this. A great deal of work has been produced which is excellent in technique but altogether lacking in beauty, owing to the use of unsuitable materials and badly selected colours.

4. The value of experiment should not be overlooked. If the best educational use is to be made of a course of weaving, a considerable amount of time will be spent on work which produces no tangible result.

This applies particularly to hand-spinning in the early stages, to experiments in dyeing with vegetable dyes, and also to the improvisation and invention of looms and equipment.

5. Pupils should be interested in the historical, geographical, and sociological associations of the craft, as illustrated in the history of weaving, the evolution of the loom, the work of primitive weavers of today, the growth and preparation of weaving materials, and the work of factories and mills.

Visits to museums, mills, exhibitions, and the studios of the craftsmen should be arranged wherever possible. The pupils should also have access to books dealing with various aspects of and associations with the craft.

CHAPTER XVI
Materials for Use

FOR THE YOUNGER CHILDREN

Raffia and Turabast.—Most suitable for the younger children, as they are easy to manipulate, and give scope for the making of a variety of attractive articles. Raffia, being inexpensive, is within the reach of all, and can be bought in small bundles in a variety of attractive colours, and in its natural cream colour. If preferred, the natural raffia can easily be dyed (after soaking) in the school or home. Turabast can be obtained in a selection of colours in bundles of continuous lengths.

Coarse Cotton Yarn can be used for the early experiments in weaving. It is suitable for either warp or weft, and can be used with 10 or 12 threads to the inch.

Felt strips are quite cheap, and can be used by the younger children for weaving mats (see Fig. 35).

Wool.—Coarse 4-ply wool can also be used by beginners. It can be bought in a range of delightful colours, and is specially recommended for use on cardboard looms, small braid looms, and with the coarse rigid heddles.

String or knitting cotton may be used for warp, with either raffia or coarse wool for weft.

FOR MORE ADVANCED WORK

Macramé string can be used for warps with raffia weft. It can also be used very successfully for tablet weaving, e.g. belts, girdles, etc.

Wool.—2- or 3-ply wool is best for finer weaving on the braid, table, or foot-power looms. Single-ply wool should only be used for weft. Ply means a bend or fold, from the French word *plier*, which means to fold. Therefore, 2-ply wool has two folds or strands twisted together, 3-ply three folds, 4-ply four folds, etc. The strand may be either loosely or tightly twisted together. The tighter the twist the greater the strength: the looser the twist the less the strength. In order to stand the strain on the loom, a tightly twisted wool should always be used for a warp. It is necessary to have a system of numbering for all kinds of yarn, by which the different sizes or thicknesses can be designated, and to provide a weaver with the means of calculating the amount of yarn required for weaving any given length of cloth.

There is a great variety in the yarn numbering systems in use in different districts, not only in respect of different fibres but also in respect of the same fibre, e.g. in wool the West of England, the Yorkshire Skein, and the Aberdeen scale are entirely different. All systems fall, however, into two distinct classes, viz. (1) Fixed weight systems, (2) Fixed length systems; the former being the more usual one adopted. In this the count is determined by the length in yards contained in any given weight—generally stated as the number of hanks in a fixed weight, viz. 1 lb. so that the thick yarns have low numbers and the finer yarns the higher numbers.

1. *In Cotton Yarn*, the hank is 840 yards long and the number of hanks in 1 lb. is the count of the yarn. Thus, if there are 20 hanks (each 840 yards long) in 1 lb. the yarn is 20 counts or 20's. 16's means 16 hanks to 1 lb.

In yarn composed of more than one thread, the number of threads twisted together is indicated alongside the original counts. Thus 2/16's means that two threads of 16 counts have been plied together, giving half the number of hanks, i.e., 8 hanks (each 840 yards long) to 1 lb. Therefore, 4/16's = 4 threads plied together, reducing the number of hanks to 4 per lb.

If 2/16's cotton is mentioned in a catalogue a weaver can easily calculate the number of yards per pound and thus ascertain the length of yarn required for any given piece of woven fabric. It has already been explained that 2/16's equals 8 hanks (of 840 yards each) to 1 lb.

$$\therefore \text{ 1 lb. of 2/16's yarn} = 840 \times 8 = 6{,}720 \text{ yards per lb.}$$
$$\tfrac{1}{4} \text{ lb.} = \frac{6720}{4} = 1{,}680 \text{ yards.}$$

The amount of cotton required for a given piece of material can be ascertained in the following way:

Required width of material $\times$ the number of threads per inch $\times$ the required length of warp.

Then, knowing the length of cotton in 1 lb., it is easy to calculate the weight of cotton needed.

To take an easy example:

For a warp 30 inches wide with 28 threads to the inch and 2 yards long, the amount of yarn required is:

$$(30 \times 28 \times 2) \text{ yards} = 1{,}680 \text{ yards.}$$

As already discovered, there are exactly 1,680 yards in $\tfrac{1}{4}$ lb. of 2/16's cotton.

Approximately the same amount is required for the weft.

The table below indicates the different lengths of the hank for the various types of yarn.

Material	Length per Hank
Cotton	840 yards.
Woollen (Yorks)	256 ,,
Linen	300 ,,
Silk	1,000 ,,

As previously stated, the counts are indicated by the number of hanks to 1 lb. (with the exception of silk—in which case the counts are indicated by the number of hanks each 1,000 yards long in 1 oz.).

To find the length of yarn in 1 lb., multiply the number of yards in one hank by the counts indicated by the supplier.

2. *In Linen Yarn*, the hank = 300 yards.

No. of hanks per lb. − counts.

40's = 40 hanks per lb.

2/40's = 20 hanks per lb.

∴ 1 lb. linen 2/40's = 300 × 20

= 6,000 yards.

A warp 30 in. wide, 25 threads per inch, will need 30 × 25 = 750 threads. As 1 lb. linen is approximately 6,000 yards it will make a warp

$$\frac{6000}{750} = 8 \text{ yards in length.}$$

∴ $\frac{1}{4}$ lb. linen will make a warp 2 yards long. An approximate amount should be allowed for weft.

3. *In Raw Silk*, 1,000 yards = 1 oz.

The number of hanks in 1 oz. = the counts.

10's = 10 hanks per oz.

30's = 30 hanks per oz.

1 oz. of 30's silk (fine) = 30,000 yards.

A warp 30 inches, 50 threads per inch, will need 30 × 50 = 1,500 threads.

∴ 1 oz. of fine silk will make a warp $\frac{30,000}{1,500}$ = 20 yards long.

Spun silk is reckoned on the same basis as cotton in all single yarn but in plied yarns the number of threads is written after the actual count of the resultant yarn. Thus 60/2 means that the yarn is actually 60's counts (with 60 hanks to the pound weight) and is composed of two threads of finer counts.

4. As the method of ascertaining the counts for wool varies so considerably amongst the manufacturers in the various parts of the country, it is impossible for a weaver to purchase wool of any particular count and from it calculate the length of warp required, unless she knows which system of counts has been adopted.

A few of the systems are indicated below purely as a matter of interest to weavers.

(1) In the Dewsbury system the yards per ounce indicates the 'counts'.

(2) In the Halifax system the weight in drams of 80 yards of yarn is the count. If 80 yards of yarn weigh 10 drams, the yarn is 10's counts and is spoken of as 10 dram yarn.

(3) In the Leeds and Huddersfield system the number of yards in 1 dram indicates the 'counts'. Thus 30's skein wool means that 30 yards will weigh 1 dram.

(4) In the West of England system, the Snap is 320 yards and the number of snaps in 1 lb. is the count.

Some suppliers of wool indicate the approximate yardage per hank, but if this is not given a weaver can calculate for herself the approximate length of wool in a hank and from this ascertain the amount of wool required for any particular warp.

It may be found that there are slight differences in the thickness of 2-ply, 3-ply wool, etc., supplied by the different makers, so the quantities given below must be taken as approximate. They should, however, give the weaver some assistance in calculating the quantity of wool required for different purposes, number of threads to the inch, etc., and experience will give greater confidence in deciding these points. When determining the amount required for warp and weft, allowance must be made for shrinking, i.e., the contraction of the threads on removing the weaving from the loom and the further process of shrinking which is necessary for the material to be practical in wear. It is also necessary to add sufficient length on to the warp for tying it on to the loom, as mentioned later in this chapter.

1. *2-ply Wool*—suitable for a scarf, runner, etc.:
   240 yards, approximately, in 1 ounce.
   Reed, 14 dents to the inch. (A 12 reed can be used if a looser texture is desired.)
   Width, 20 inches.
   Number of threads required, $14 \times 20 = 280$.
   The amount of wool required to make a warp of 280 threads, 1 yard
   long $= \dfrac{\text{No. of threads in warp}}{\text{No. of yards in 1 ounce}} = \dfrac{280}{240} = 1\frac{1}{6}$ ounces.

From this the weaver can calculate the length of warp made by 1 ounce of wool if the material is to be 30 inches wide; also length of warp using a 16 dent reed—20 inches wide.

2. *3-ply Wool*:
   1 ounce = 175 yards, approximately.
   12 reed, 20 inches wide = 240 threads.
   Length of warp which can be made from 1 ounce of wool =
   $\dfrac{\text{Total length of wool in 1 ounce}}{\text{Total number of threads in the warp}} = \dfrac{175}{240} = \frac{3}{4}$ yard long (approx.)

From this can be calculated the length of warp made by 1 ounce of wool, using a finer reed, greater width, etc.

In addition to 2-ply and 3-ply wool, plain or mercerised cotton, rayon, silk, etc., there are many other fancy materials on the market. These lend variety to many woven fabrics.

Descriptions of some of these fancy yarns are given below and some of them are shown in Fig. 23.

Curl or Loop Yarn is made by turning a comparatively thick thread around a much finer ground thread so as to form a succession of curls or loops along the surface of the yarn.

Gimp Yarn is produced by twisting a fine thread round a thick soft thread or vice versa.

Snarl Yarn is made from very hard twisted yarn, which is allowed to form kinks or curly places in the thread at intervals.

Knop Yarn is a two-fold yarn and is produced on a machine with an intermittent motion which stops the progress of the yarn while one simple thread twists round the foundation thread to form a knop.

Slub Yarn is produced by twisting a fine thread with another thread, in which at intervals a soft place termed a 'slub' has been formed.

Lurex. This is a non-tarnishable metal thread obtainable in various colours, including silver and gold, but it should be used very sparingly to give the best effect.

Yarn for Tweed. The thickness of the yarn is indicated by the term 'cut'. According to the Sutherland method, 1 lb. of '1' cut yarn measures 200 yards approximately.

From these figures, the length of the other 'cuts' can be calculated, e.g.:

1 lb. of 9 'cut' yarn .. 200 × 9 .. 1,800 yards
1 lb. of 11 'cut' yarn .. 200 × 11 .. 2,200 yards.
1 lb. of 16 'cut' yarn .. 200 × 16 .. 3,200 yards.

The yarn most generally used is 9 'cut' for a heavy tweed; 11 'cut' for a lighter weight material; 16 'cut' for a material still lighter in weight.

These tweed yarns should be used as follows:

Cut		Warp
9	..	16 threads per inch (Tabby)
		18 ,, ,, ,, (Twill)
11	..	18 ,, ,, ,, (Tabby)
		20 ,, ,, ,, (Twill)
16	..	22 ,, ,, ,, (Tabby)
		24 ,, ,, ,, (Twill)

The number of 'picks' (rows of weft) per inch varies in accordance with the beat, but the average number of 'picks' per inch for 11 'cut' yarn is 16 for tabby and 20 for twill. A coarser reed should be used in each case, putting two threads per dent to avoid the undue friction likely to be caused by the use of a fine reed with one thread per dent.

As a rough guide the *total* amount of yarn required for each yard of material is approximately $\frac{3}{4}$ lb. A warp 32/33 in. wide should be put on the loom in order to weave a fabric 27/29 in. in width (after shrinkage) and 3 in. to 4 in. allowed for shrinkage in each yard in length and slightly less for shrinkage in width.

The following lengths of material (after shrinking and finishing) are necessary for various garments:

Man's suit	..	$7\frac{1}{2}$ yards.
Man's sports coat	..	4 yards.
Woman's costume	..	6 to $6\frac{1}{2}$ yards.
Woman's coat	..	6 to $6\frac{1}{2}$ yards.
Woman's skirt	..	3 yards.

To calculate the Length of Warp for a Foot-power Loom.

Decide on the length of material required, e.g. 6 yards long. To this must be added 3–4 inches for every yard for shrinkage; also $\frac{3}{4}$ yard for wastage on the loom for tying on at front—and the amount left on back roller (smaller looms will need much less than this). See Chapters VIII and X. Therefore, if the finished material must be 6 yards, the length of warp should be 6 yards, plus $\frac{3}{4}$ yard for shrinkage, plus $\frac{3}{4}$ yard for wastage $= 7\frac{1}{2}$ yards. Allow 4 inches in width for shrinkage, e.g.:

Material, 36 inches wide.
Shrinkage, 4 inches.
Result, 32 inches.

Woven material is shrunk by well steaming and pressing, thereby closing up the fibres and giving it a more finished appearance. It must be done thoroughly to avoid any further shrinkage after making up.

Tweeds need very special attention. This is given in detail at the end of Chapter XII on the Weaving of Tweeds.

MAKING UP HAND-WOVEN MATERIAL

This is an important side of the work and should receive careful attention. Many really good pieces of woven material have been ruined by careless or unsuitable treatment. Simple decorative stitchery can be used quite successfully, as shown on the bags, Figs. 49a and 49b. Each of the bags has been made by joining several woven strips decoratively.

The runner for the bag, Fig. 49a, has been made by several woven bands, under which the cord passes, whilst the cord in the bag, Fig. 49b, passes through slots made in the crochet border at the top.

Bags should be lined with material of a suitable texture and the use of ornate silky materials discouraged.

Scarves can have a knotted fringe or be hemstitched. The latter can be done more easily while the scarf is on the loom and the warp threads taut. It is done in the usual way by passing the needle round a group of threads; again round the same group of threads, but this time passing the needle through a small piece of the woven material in addition. If, however, a hemstitched hem is required this can be done in one of two ways:

(1) By inserting a thick thread in one of the sheds of the weaving, at the right distance needed for the depth of the hem. When the weaving is completed the hem can be turned down and tacked in line with this coarse thread. This can then be easily withdrawn a few inches at a time as the actual hemstitching proceeds. See Fig. 167;

or

(2) The weaving should be done in the usual way, then one thread should be drawn out and the hem folded and tacked down to this line (too many threads should not be removed as the material would be weakened). It is generally sufficient to remove two threads, but as hand-woven material is loose in texture, the weaver will find it more satisfactory to draw the second thread out a few inches at a time while the hemstitching is in progress.

Special attention should be given to fastenings. Weavers are often inclined to use press studs and zip fasteners for hand-woven pochettes, etc.—when a woven strip, under which the flap could be passed, would be much more in keeping with the fabric. Cords, flat plaits (see Fig. 10), strips of tablet weaving or narrow hand-woven braids, are useful for trimmings, and plain wooden buttons or button moulds decorated with simple stitchery make suitable fastenings. A good fastening for a pochette can be made from a piece of material rolled as a cylinder (see Fig. 36).

As hand-woven material is inclined to fray it is better to overcast any edges if the material is to be put away for a time. This can be done quite easily while the material is on the loom. If a garment is to be made it is advisable to overcast the edges as each piece is cut out, or, in the case of neck or sleeve edges, to run a loose row of machining in order to prevent undue stretching. Alternatively, a row of machine stitching can be run round each section of the pattern before cutting the material.

Weavers need not hesitate to cut hand-woven material if they carry out the aforementioned precautions. Hand-woven garments need not be shapeless. The material can be used in the same way as machine-woven fabric, if handled in the right way.

All materials need careful pressing with a fairly hot iron, over a damp cloth.

216

BIBLIOGRAPHY

PRIMITIVE WEAVING AND SPINNING

Primitive Looms. H. Ling Roth. Bankfield Museum, Halifax
Bankfield Museum Notes. H. Ling Roth
  No. 2. *Ancient Egyptian and Greek Looms*
  No. 12. *Methods of Hand Spinning in Egypt and the Sudan.* Grace M. Crowfoot
History and Principles of Weaving. Barlow
Dictionary of Greek and Roman Antiquities. Smith. MURRAY. 2 vols.
Ancient Egyptians. Wilkinson
Encyclopaedia Biblica
Textrinum Antiquorum. Yates
Reports of the U.S.A. National Museum
The Origin of Inventions. Mason
The Technical Arts and Sciences of the Ancients. Albert Neuburger. METHUEN
Indian Blankets and their Makers. George Wharton James. TUDOR PUBLISHING CO.
A Short History of Decorative Textiles and Tapestries. Violetta Thurstan. PEPLER AND SEWELL
Ancient Decorative Textiles. Violetta Thurstan. FAVIL PRESS

DYEING

Vegetable Dyes. E. Mairet. FABER AND FABER
The Use of Vegetable Dyes. Violetta Thurstan. DRYAD PRESS
Notes on Spinning and Dyeing Wool. M. Holding
Scouring and Dyeing with Vegetable Dye Recipes. K. Grasett. LONDON SCHOOL OF WEAVING
Vegetable Dyeing for Beginners. Byrtha L. Stavert. No. 41 Creative Handicrafts Series
  MACMILLAN
Your Yarn Dyeing. Elsie Davenport. SYLVAN PRESS

SPINNING

Complete Guide to Hand Spinning. K. Grasett. LONDON SCHOOL OF WEAVING
Spinning Wool. Leaflet No. 83. DRYAD PRESS
Hand Carding and Spinning of Wool. Alice Borden. No. 29, Creative Handicrafts Series
  MACMILLAN

WEAVING

Handloom Weaving. Luther Hooper. PITMAN
Weaving for Beginners. Luther Hooper. PITMAN
Foot Power Loom Weaving. E. F. Worst. BRUCE PUBLISHING CO.
How to Weave Linen. E. F. Worst. BRUCE PUBLISHING CO.
The Shuttlecraft Book of American Hand-weaving. M. Atwater. MACMILLAN
Embroidery and Tapestry Weaving. A. H. Christie. PITMAN
Weaving and Pattern Drafting. K. Grasett. LONDON SCHOOL OF WEAVING
Notes on Carpet Knotting and Weaving. C. E. C. Tattersall. VICTORIA AND ALBERT MUSEUM
The Romance of French Weaving. Paul Rodier. TUDOR PUBLISHING CO.
Handweaving To-day. Ethel Mairet. FABER AND FABER
Weaving for Amateurs. Helen Coates. STUDIO
Weaving Patterns. Violetta Thurstan. LONDON SCHOOL OF WEAVING
A Key to Weaving. Mary S. Black. BRUCE PUBLISHING CO.
Simple Tartan Weaving. A. MacDonald. DRYAD PRESS
A Handweaver's Pattern Book. M. P. Davison. Published by the author at Swarthmore,
  Pennsylvania

Pennsylvania German Home Weaving. M. P. Davison. Published by the author at Swarthmore, Pennsylvania
Scandinavian Art Weaving. Elmer W. Hickman. Published by the author at Emlenton, Pa.
Notes on Weaving Techniques. Florence E. House. ARTS COOPERATIVE SERVICE, NEW YORK
Weave Your Own Tweeds. Roger Millen. DAVISON, SWARTHMORE
Foundations of Fabric Structure. John H. Strong
Handbok i Veving. C. Halvorsen. J. W. CAPPELENS FORLAG, OSLO
Vaev selv. G. D. Jespersen and M. M. Jornung. J. GJELLERUPS FORLAG, COPENHAGEN
Uber Brettchenweberei. (Tablet Weaving). M. Lehmann-Filhes. DIETRICH REIMER, BERLIN
Card Loom Weaving. Leaflet No. 100. DRYAD PRESS
Tablet Weaving. Leaflet No. 111. DRYAD PRESS
Hand-Weaving on Two-way Looms. Leaflet No. 91. DRYAD PRESS
Weaving on Four-way Table Looms. Leaflet No. 89. DRYAD PRESS
Dryad Foot Power Looms. Leaflet No. 90. DRYAD PRESS
Rug Weaving. Leaflet No. 85. DRYAD PRESS
Hand Weaving. Lotte Becher. STUDIO
Designing on the Loom. Mary Kirby. STUDIO
A Handweaver's Workbook. Heather G. Thorpe. MACMILLAN, NEW YORK
Weaving Patterns. Malin Selander. WEZATA FORLAG, GOTEBORG
Weaving Patterns for the Two-way Loom. Vera Miles. DRYAD PRESS
Practical Four-shaft Weaving. Vera Miles. DRYAD PRESS

COLOUR

Suggestions for the Study of Colour. H. Barrett Carpenter
Colour Sense Training and Colour Using. E. J. Taylor. BLACKIE
The Enjoyment and Use of Colour. W. Sargent. SCRIBNER
Textile Design and Colour. Wm. Watson. LONGMANS, GREEN

MISCELLANEOUS

The Linen Trade of Europe. John Horner. MCCAW, STEVENSON AND ORR, BELFAST
Yarn and Cloth Making. Mary Lois Kissell. MACMILLAN
The Story of Clothes. M. and M. Petersham. DENT
Fabrics. Grace G. Denny. J. B. LIPPINCOTT
Athene (quarterly magazine). SOCIETY FOR EDUCATION THROUGH ART
Handweaving and Education. Ethel Mairet. FABER AND FABER
Irish Linen, Queen of Fabrics. IRISH LINEN GUILD
Sheep Farming. Young Farmers' Club Booklet No. 16
Sheep. Thomas. FABER AND FABER
Lagan Valley, 1800–1850. Green. (History of an Irish Linen Manufacturer)
So Spins the Silkworm. Zoe, Lady Hart Dyke. ROCKLIFFE
The Heritage of Cotton. Crawford. FAIRCHILD PUBLISHING CO. (*The* book on cotton's history)
Homecraft in Sweden. Maj. Sterner. F. LEWIS LTD.
The Ashley Book of Knots. C. W. Ashley. FABER AND FABER
The Story Book of Rayon*
The Story Book of Cotton
The Story Book of Silk   M. and M. Petersham. WELLS GARDNER
The Story Book of Wool
The Wools of Britain. Ella McLeod (Haigh & Newton). PITMAN
*(Lithographed picture books for Junior School age)

Index